What is Philosophy of Language?

What is Philosophy of Language?

Claudine Verheggen

polity

First published in 2026 by Polity Press Ltd.

Polity Press Ltd.
65 Bridge Street
Cambridge CB2 1UR, UK

Polity Press Ltd.
111 River Street
Hoboken, NJ 07030, USA

ISBN-13: 978-1-5095-5696-0
ISBN-13: 978-1-5095-5697-7 (pb)

A catalogue record for this book is available from the British Library.

Library of Congress Control Number: 2025949902

Typeset in 11 on 13pt Sabon
by Cheshire Typesetting Ltd, Cuddington, Cheshire
Printed and bound in Great Britain by Ashford Colour Ltd

For further information on Polity, visit our website:
politybooks.com

For my students

Contents

Acknowledgements

I am immensely grateful to Robert Myers, Olivia Sultanescu, and Christopher Campbell for their careful comments on, and invaluable discussion of, the entire manuscript. I also want to thank the editorial team at Polity for their patience and support during the preparation of the manuscript, as well as two anonymous referees for their insightful and constructive feedback. Finally, thanks are due to Nathan Malcomson for his help with the bibliography and the index.

1

Introduction

This book is a concise introduction to the philosophy of language, the central concept of which I take to be that of linguistic meaning. The book is designed for any philosophy student and any philosophically minded person who is interested in language and wishes to become acquainted with its philosophical aspects and with what some of the most prominent philosophers in the field have said about them. But what are the philosophical aspects of language, and what reasons might the philosophy student and the philosophically minded person have to be interested in them?

1.1 What are the philosophical aspects of language?

Answering this question is really the main task of this book. Still, a succinct, preliminary answer may be in order. Obviously, philosophy of language is a branch of philosophy, and our understanding of what philosophy is therefore shapes, at least to some extent, our understanding of what philosophy of language is. The question what philosophy is can itself be a philosophical question, the answer to which, like the answers to most philosophical questions, commands no consensus. Still, in line with this lack of consensus, many philosophers agree that what makes philosophy worth pursuing is the kind of inquiry it engages in, the relentless questioning, revising, and refining of philosophical positions. The critical nature of this process is perfectly compatible with making progress, as we shall see in this book. But, more often than not, what is rewarding in philosophy is more the process than the result; for it is in the process that the problems examined get to be better understood and the complexities of the issues they involve get to be unravelled – two enterprises that teach us something about ourselves and the world around us. Now, other fields of inquiry, while perhaps not favouring the process over the result to the same degree, may exhibit these characteristics as well. What, then, makes philosophy different?

As I see it, philosophy attempts to answer questions that no other field of inquiry is in a position to answer, at least not in the same way. This is not to say that proper answers to philosophical questions simply ignore the findings of other fields, or that researchers in these fields simply ignore philosophical endeavours that may be connected to their own work. Thus, in pairs such as philosophy of mind and psychology, philosophy of language and linguistics, philosophy of knowledge and natural science, the two components may inform each other, but philosophy always digs more deeply, so to speak.

Here is a simple example. Science, and common sense for that matter, presuppose that many of the beliefs we have about the world around us are based on our sensory experiences. Thus we believe that the tower at the end of the street is round because round is the way it looks to us. Of course, we may be wrong about this, for example if it is a foggy day and the tower is far away. Still, we are able to distinguish, without too much difficulty, between those cases in which our senses are to be trusted and those in which they are not. Similarly, the scientist is able to distinguish between the superficial properties of a natural kind – say, water – and its fundamental nature – say, its chemical composition – by means of technical instruments. The point, though, is that in each case the senses are invoked and taken to be reliable, once the most favourable conditions of perception are taken to be present. This is precisely the point that the philosopher of knowledge calls into question. She asks: what reason do we have to believe that our senses are ever reliable, that it is not the case that all our experiences and thoughts and beliefs, seemingly about the world around us, are compatible with none of them being veridical or true, so that we have no knowledge of the world around us after all? I shall not go into the possible answers to those questions here. Suffice it to say that the philosopher of knowledge has to address them, somehow.

What I am trying to suggest is that philosophers inquire into the fundamental nature of phenomena, especially human phenomena. Thus, to continue with my example, the philosopher of knowledge asks not merely whether the conditions taken to justify a belief are fulfilled on a particular occasion, but whether fulfilling these conditions ever leads to justified belief and so to knowledge. Similarly, the philosopher of language does not ask merely what the meanings of particular sentences are, or how the grammatical form of sentences may affect their meaning, as the linguist may ask; she asks what makes it possible for those sentences to have meaning and to mean what they do to begin with. This is the fundamental question the philosopher of language is concerned with. However, this question, as we shall see, generates a flurry of others, some of which need to be addressed in order to answer the fundamental one, while others cannot be answered properly until we have an answer to the fundamental one. Later in this introduction, when I sketch the structure of the book, I will mention the central questions I have in mind. Note for now the dimension of generality, which is also characteristic of philosophy. The philosopher of language does not study the features of any particular natural language, such as English or Basque, but what all such languages have in common. What fundamentally explains what it is for the words of English to have meaning applies to the words of Basque as well.

1.2   What reasons might one have to be interested in the philosophical aspects of language?

First, there is the sheer wonder at what makes sounds and inscriptions produced by human beings meaningful in a way in which the very same sounds, when produced randomly by the wind, or the very same inscriptions, when appearing randomly in the sand, cannot be. We are so accustomed to understanding each other, provided that we share a language, that we may have lost, or simply not share, this sense of wonder. But we may recover or acquire it if we reflect on the experience we have when we encounter a language that is totally foreign to us: the sounds we hear make no sense to us, they are just noises, but if we notice someone understanding them and responding to them, it may look to us as if a magical trick had been performed. The philosopher of language aims to explain why no magic is involved in this achievement, and yet its absence need not take away the wonder.

Second, as already suggested, philosophy of language is the philosophical study of natural languages such as English or Basque, the kind of languages used by human beings. (This does not rule out the possibility that other beings have languages that exhibit the same level of complexity as that of human languages. But our inquiry here is based on the languages we are familiar with.) Language is a major part of what makes us distinctively human. We attach meaning to sounds and inscriptions in order to communicate with one another, to inform others about the world, including about ourselves, and to become informed about the world and about others. Through language we exchange reports about current events, such as the wildfires burning near Athens, or about current states of affairs, such as the kind of wine there is in the fridge, or about our states of mind, such as fearing that the fires will last or hoping that they will not, or believing that there is some chardonnay in the fridge, or longing for a glass of wine. Through language we make things happen, such as convincing our friend not to go near Athens, or getting a glass of chardonnay. Through language we mislead, deceive, praise, blame, insult, hurt, impress, convince, encourage, joke, create poetry and fiction. Imagine what we would be like without language! So, it is in itself interesting to figure out what makes it possible for our words to have meaning and so for us to have a first language. It teaches us something about ourselves.

Third, precisely because language offers such a unique way for us to learn about and act upon the world around us, the philosophical study of language, the study of what makes it possible, is also interesting because scrutinizing these connections promises to help to illuminate the multifarious aspects of the world around us, both from a theoretical and from a more practical point of view. Thus the philosophical study of language may help us to understand what the world is made of, as well as our reactions and attitudes towards it, thereby again shedding light on us.

Fourth, the philosophical study of language is interesting in part because the meaning of sentences is closely connected to the content of the beliefs, desires, and other states of mind we express by using them. These notions play a central role in the study of the mind (what is it for the human mind to have the distinctive kinds of beliefs and desires it has?) and in the study of ethics (what sorts of beliefs do we have about how to act, and how are they related to our desires?). The notion of belief, in particular, is also central to the philosophical study of knowledge. On most understandings of what knowledge is, belief is a crucial element of the state of knowing. Thus, if we are not clear about what makes words mean what they do, we may not be clear about what makes the states of mind we express linguistically have the contents they have, and hence we may not be in a position to tackle many philosophical problems that, on the face of it, are not intrinsically connected to language. To go back to my example, if we are not clear about the nature of belief, of what it is for a belief to have the content it has – and beliefs are identified and distinguished from one another by their content – we may not be able to address the sceptic who calls into question the reliability of our senses as grounds for our beliefs about the world around us.

Fifth, the philosophical study of language and of its cognate states of mind may also shed light on other fields, such as psychology and cognitive science on the one hand (by asking, say, what the connections are between having a language and thinking as we do) and political, social, and legal theory on the other (by asking, say, how words such as 'democracy', or 'gender', or 'contract' come to mean what they do, or how words come to have a derogatory meaning).

This book assumes no knowledge of philosophy, let alone philosophy of language. It also avoids any unnecessary philosophical jargon (any unavoidable jargon will be clearly introduced). As I see it, philosophy of language, which, I know from experience, often intimidates students, can be just as accessible as any other philosophical field. As I always tell my students, its subject matter may be more familiar to us than any other philosophical subject matter. For we all know how to speak, how to use language to communicate, but we do not all know much about, say, art, or law, or physics, which may make the philosophical study of those fields difficult, if not impossible, for some. In fact, it may be because we are so familiar with language that we are puzzled as to how to approach it philosophically. We know how to use language to describe, say, the state of the fridge, to express, say, our hope that it will be sunny in Toronto tomorrow, or our worry about the wildfires burning near Athens, and so on and so forth. In short, we know how to connect language with the extralinguistic world. All the same, one important philosophical question is, how do such connections get established? How do words come to have the meanings that connect them to bits of reality, indeed, any meaning at all?

1.3 The structure of the book

The approach embraced in the book is both thematic and historical. We'll start in the second chapter by isolating the central notion of meaning that is to be elucidated. As we'll see, the notion of linguistic meaning may be ambiguous even if it is clear to us that it is to be distinguished from the notion of, say, the meaning of life or the meaning of art. Suffice it for now to mention the ambiguity of the question: 'What do you mean?' When asking it, are we wondering about the meaning of the words the speaker used, or about the purpose of the speaker in using those words? We'll then look at the questions that initially motivated philosophical accounts of meaning. We'll see how the accounts provided to answer these questions themselves generated new problems, and how addressing them little by little led to the development of more and more mature and complex accounts of meaning. We might think of the questions that have been addressed by philosophers of language – especially in the past 130 years, when most progress has been made – as falling into two broad categories, one having to do with the relation between meaning and extralinguistic reality, the other having to do with the relation between meaning and language users and their use of language. As we'll see, philosophers initially focused on the former category. But, as more and more questions arose, it became urgent to ask what the connection is between the two sets of questions, and whether the former can in fact be addressed properly only by also addressing the latter.

Early attempts at answering the question what it is for words to mean what they do will be examined in the third chapter. A natural place to look for the source of meaning is the minds of speakers. Accordingly, it has been maintained that words come to mean what they do because they are somehow connected to something mental – say, mental images or ideas. Another natural place to look is the world of objects and events surrounding us. Here the thought is that the items we talk about are themselves the source of the meanings of our words, and that these words are somehow associated with those items. Both these views, however, generate all kinds of problems. To mention two central ones, first, there is the question of what makes it the case that a given item, be it internal or external, generates the meaning that it allegedly does. What is it about, say, a mental image or a sample of green that makes it the case that the word 'green' means *green* rather than, say, *leaf* (since the image or sample may also be of a leaf)? Furthermore, the idea that entities in the world all by themselves determine the meanings of some words generates puzzles that were first introduced and addressed by the philosophers who first put language on a firm philosophical ground. How could, for instance, two names for the same person – 'Ruth Rendell' and

'Barbara Vine', or 'Mark Twain' and 'Samuel Clemens' – have the same 'meaning' and this be unknown to someone competent with these names?

In the fourth chapter we examine more recent and more sophisticated answers to the question what it is for words to mean what they do. All these answers focus on items that are external to speakers as the alleged source of meaning. The views we'll examine, however, though they have much more to say in defence of the claim that words mean what they do because of some sort of direct connection between them and items in the environment of the speakers who use them, still fail in the end fully to answer the question how the relevant connections get established and maintained.

This leads us in the fifth chapter to reconsider how we should think of the connection between language and extralinguistic reality. Chapter 4 will have discussed attempts to 'externalize' meaning, in that, at least for words that are about external entities such as people or cities, or objects such as trees, or properties such as colours, the source of their meaning is not said to be items in the mind of speakers who use them but the external items they are about. Accordingly, we will have focused up to that point on the relation between particular entities or properties in the world and the words we use to talk about them. But the difficulties these externalist views encountered suggest that we should perhaps focus instead on the relation between *states of affairs* and *events* that occur in the world (rather than objects and properties in the world) and the *sentences* we use to talk about them. After all, we are interested in reflecting on language in part because we are interested in the distinctly human ways we communicate through it. And, normally, it is sentences we utter to communicate linguistically, to provide information about the world and about one another, to express our wishes, hopes, fears, and so on. Normally, in short, it is sentences we utter to get things done. This opens up another way of externalizing meaning, which also introduces a concept that may play an indispensable role in the answer to our fundamental question: the concept of truth. For, to put it very roughly, if sentences are to be connected with states of affairs such as there being chardonnay in the fridge, or with events such as wildfires burning near Athens, then they are to be connected with what may be the case or may be happening, that is, in short, with what may make them true. This, however, still does not fully answer the question how the connections between language and extralinguistic reality are established. The next two chapters investigate how we may improve on this answer.

Up to this point we will have tried to answer our fundamental question by considering exclusively matters that fall in the first broad category: could words' meaning what they do, and so their ability to hook onto the world, be explained simply by appealing to the mental states, however characterized, of speakers, or simply by appealing to features, however characterized, of the world around them? In the third chapter we briefly considered the minds of speakers as potential sources of meaning and, in the fifth, we considered the relation between meaning and extralinguistic reality through the lenses of communication. But up to this point we will have paid little attention to language users themselves, to their take or perspective on what goes on when they use words meaningfully, and thus to our second broad category of questions. However, when people use words meaningfully, they do so with some understanding of what they are doing; they do so meaning it, as it is tempting to say, and not haphazardly. This suggests that there must be something about language users that explains their linguistic behaviour and that perhaps constitutes their meaning what they mean by their words. In the sixth chapter we examine a powerful attempt to show that nothing of the sort is to be found in language users, which leads to the radical claim that, even though there are reasons to ascribe meaning to people's utterances, these ascriptions are never true. Strictly speaking, people never mean anything by any of their linguistic expressions. But surely, this cannot be right.

In the seventh and last chapter we examine what has gone wrong, which, in a nutshell, is our focusing on the relation between meaning and language users to the detriment of the relation between meaning and extralinguistic reality (rather than the other way around, as we did in the previous chapters). What we will have failed to consider up to this point is language as it is used by people in given circumstances and what it is about their use that makes language possible in the first place. In short, we will have failed to consider language *in use*, language users *qua users*. Repairing this failure is the goal of this chapter, which will suggest that the problems incurred by trying to answer the first set of questions, concerning words' ability to hook onto the world, cannot be solved without answering the second set, concerning language users' ability to use words with understanding and purpose. Fulfilling this goal will involve considering new questions. What kinds of use are we supposed to focus on? Whose use are we supposed to consider, the use of individual speakers or that of groups or communities? Indeed, could an individual who has been socially isolated for life have a language, or is language an essentially social phenomenon? What is the role, if any, of linguistic conventions in determining what we mean by our words?

1.4 What this book is not about

There are several things this book is not about, even some things that pertain to the philosophy of language.

To begin with, this is a book in the analytic tradition, a tradition that was in fact inaugurated by the philosophers of language who posed the puzzles that will initially guide our inquiry. Thus it will not discuss continental and non-western approaches to the philosophy of language. Furthermore, this book addresses foundational issues in philosophy of language. Thus it will not discuss issues related to political or social philosophy or, more generally, what has come to be called 'applied philosophy of language'. Discussing such matters, even at an introductory level, would in fact require another book.

I won't pretend that the picture of philosophy of language I am presenting here is the only one that could be provided. I have chosen to emphasize some issues rather than others, as well as some philosophical positions rather than others. I have chosen those that strike me as most interesting and most compelling and that I have thought most about. Relatedly, I won't discuss, or even mention, all the views of the philosophers I have chosen to cover in order to introduce those issues and positions. (Nor will I discuss all the possible interpretations of the views I have chosen to cover.) Thus, I also won't pretend that the book presents a totally detached or 'neutral', let alone complete, picture of what philosophy of language is all about, even when the focus is on foundational issues. Such a presentation would in any case require not a short book but an encyclopaedia. But what I have tried to present is a narrative, which yields a constant motivation for the reader to keep reading by making her wonder indeed what happens next, how a given problem is going to be solved, and what further problems the solution might generate. References to the texts discussed will be given at the end of each chapter, followed by suggestions for further readings, both on the texts discussed and on some of the positions and issues not covered.

Glossary

From now on, I will often use the word 'speaker' to talk about language users in general. What I say applies equally to spoken, written, or signed languages.

When I say something about a word or expression or, as it is said in philosophical jargon, when I mention a word or expression, I put it in quotation marks (e.g. 'speaker' has seven letters). Of course, when I report someone's word or expression, I also put it in quotation marks (e.g. she said: 'Many speakers participated in the conference').

I often use 'word' and 'expression' interchangeably, to refer simply to a potentially meaningful linguistic unit; expressions, though, can consist of more than one word, indeed, can be entire sentences.

When a word stands for its meaning, I italicize it, as in 'speaker' means *speaker*.

A useful distinction often made by philosophers of language is the distinction between token and type. We can talk about types of things, for example speakers in general, or about particular instances of those types, for example the last speaker who addressed the audience. Relatedly, we can talk about types of words or tokens of words. For example, the sentence 'Yesterday's speaker performed better than today's speaker' contains six word types but seven word tokens, since it contains two tokens of the type of word 'speaker'.

Further Readings

Two excellent, more advanced introductions to the philosophy of language:

Morris, Michael. 2007. *An Introduction to the Philosophy of Language*. Cambridge University Press.
Miller, Alexander. 2018. *Philosophy of Language* (3rd edn). Routledge.

An excellent collection of primary texts:

Martinich, A. P. and David Sosa. 2012. *The Philosophy of Language* (6th edn). Oxford University Press.

On applied philosophy of language:

Khoo, Justin and Rachel Sterken (eds). 2021. *The Routledge Handbook of Social and Political Philosophy of Language*. Routledge.

Anderson, Luvell and Ernie Lepore (eds). 2024. *The Oxford Handbook of Applied Philosophy of Language*. Oxford University Press.

On what is distinctive of analytic philosophy:

Beaney, Michael. 2018. *Analytic Philosophy: A Very Short Introduction*. Oxford University Press.

Dummett, Michael. 2006. *Origins of Analytical Philosophy*. Cambridge University Press.

On the history of analytic philosophy:

Hylton, Peter. 2010. *Russell, Idealism, and the Emergence of Analytic Philosophy*. Oxford University Press.

Potter, Michael D. 2020. *The Rise of Analytic Philosophy, 1879–1930: From Frege to Ramsey*. Routledge.

The Stanford Encyclopedia of Philosophy is always a good resource for those who are looking to delve further into a topic in philosophy. Entries can be found on most of the philosophers and philosophical positions discussed in this book: https://plato.stanford.edu.

2

What is Linguistic Meaning?

The aim of this chapter is to isolate the notion of meaning that is central to the philosophy of language. As mentioned in the introduction, the kind of languages we are focusing on are natural languages such as English or Basque. We are not, however, interested in how any particular natural language functions; we are interested in what all such languages have in common. For starters, we may note some features that belong to linguistic meaning but do not belong to other phenomena we may describe as meaningful – such as the setting of the sun or the performance of a sonata – or as languages – such as the language of bees or the languages of art. Three such features seem to be fundamental.

2.1 Fundamental features of linguistic meaning

First, as already suggested, when we use expressions meaningfully, we perform actions – call them speech acts (though this term is sometimes used more narrowly: see section 2.5) – which, like all other kinds of actions, are intentional, that is, done for some reason or other (which language users may or may not be fully aware of at the time of their performance). This is what distinguishes genuine linguistic behaviour from the effects of wind or the behaviour of automata, which may appear to engage in the same use of expressions without intending to do so and thus presumably without meaning anything by them.

Second, one of the features that are distinctive of language use is that we may use words to produce utterances we have never produced before and we may understand utterances we have never heard before. Indeed, we constantly generate and grasp novel uses of language, which is what, after all, serves some of the most central and important purposes of engaging in linguistic communication: to inform others and motivate them to act in certain ways, and to get informed and be likewise motivated by them.

Third, another feature that is distinctive of language use is that the same expression may be used sometimes to say something true and sometimes to say something false, without changing the meaning of the expression. For instance, 'It is sunny in Toronto' is sometimes true, sometimes false. Indeed, it is because the expressions that make up sentences can be used incorrectly that mistakes can be made and lies can be told. Of course, some sentences, for example 'Squares have four sides', are always true, but even such sentences contain words that may be applied incorrectly, as in 'That figure is a square', when the demonstrated figure is a rectangle. The important point here is that, if words could always be said to be used correctly no matter how they are used, and so no use of words could ever be said to be incorrect, words could not be meaningful. Thus, to be meaningful, words must be governed by standards of correct application, which may be expressed, say, for 'green', as follows: if 'green' means *green*, then 'green' is applied correctly only to green things. 'Green' retains its meaning if it is used to describe a blue thing, but in that case it is applied incorrectly. The meaning we attach to words in virtue of which they can be used correctly or incorrectly is their literal meaning.

Whatever account we give of meaning, it will have to be one that explains, or at least makes room for, the three aforementioned features, which reflect the intentional, the novel, and the standard-governed nature of language use. Now that we know a little better what we are looking for, the question is: how are we supposed to start our inquiry?

2.2   An initial puzzle about meaning

I suggested in the introduction that there may be no consensus on what philosophy is. There definitely is no consensus on how to approach a philosophical question, once we have it. But here I like to follow Bertrand Russell, one of the very first analytic philosophers to investigate meaning, who said that philosophers should fill their mind with puzzles, because puzzles are to philosophy what experiments are to science. Here, then, is a puzzle we might start with, a puzzle that arises out of the clash between two commonsensical beliefs. On the one hand, we use language for all kinds of purposes we want to achieve – getting dinner, getting someone out of the way, getting the latest news about the wildfires burning near Athens. Thus it may come naturally to think that the uses to which we put the sentences we utter determine what they mean. On the other hand, it does not look as if we can specify the meanings of expressions in terms of these uses or purposes. Getting someone out of the way may be achieved by saying 'There is a snake!'; but getting someone out of the way does not tell us what 'There is a snake!' means. Indeed, the same sentence ('There is a snake!'), with the same meaning, may be uttered to achieve different kinds of purposes, such as getting someone to be frightened or distracted, and the same purpose (getting someone out of the way) may be achieved by uttering different sentences with different meanings, such as by saying 'Excuse me!' Furthermore, the same sentence, with the same meaning, can be used to make an assertion, issue a warning or an order, ask a question, and so on. For instance, 'Is there any salt?' can be uttered to ask a question or to make a request – to cite only two of the most obvious possible uses. Thus the uses to which we put the sentences we utter do not seem to determine their meaning after all. Or, at any rate, if they do, the relevant uses will have to be carefully delineated. What, then, is the relationship between meaning and all the things we do in using words? How can reflecting on this help us to get clearer about the notion of meaning?

2.3   An attempted solution to the puzzle

The British philosopher Paul Grice was one of the first philosophers of language who, in a celebrated article published in 1957, tried to shed light on the notion of linguistic meaning by focusing on the connection between speakers' utterances and the effects speakers intend to produce by uttering them. Indeed, he was one of the first philosophers to investigate meaning by paying attention to the connection between meaning and language users – that is, the connection our second broad category of questions in philosophy of language is concerned with. My primary interest at this stage is not to pursue these questions – this will be done in chapters 5–7. But it is to exploit Grice's analysis of the connection in order better to identify the notion of meaning that is the primary object of our study.

Grice starts his investigation into the nature of linguistic meaning by distinguishing it from other kinds of meaning. Thus he distinguishes between 'natural' kinds of meaning, exemplified in sentences such as 'Those spots mean measles', and 'non-natural' kinds of meaning, exemplified in sentences such as 'Those three rings on the bell (of the bus) mean that the bus is full.' Linguistic meaning, exemplified in sentences such as '"It is sunny in Toronto today" means that it is sunny in Toronto today', is a kind of non-natural meaning. What are the main differences between the two types of meaning?

The two most striking differences are connected to two of the features that we just saw to be essential to linguistic meaning. First, whereas 'Those spots mean measles' entails the presence of measles – the spots could not be present without measles being present – 'Those three rings on the bell mean that the bus is full' does not entail that the bus is in fact full whenever those three rings are struck. The bus conductor could be mistaken. Likewise, '"It is sunny today in Toronto" means that it is sunny today in Toronto' does not entail that it is sunny in Toronto whenever the sentence is uttered. The speaker could be misinformed, or lying. This is connected to what I called earlier (p. 17) the standard-governed feature of meaning: linguistic expressions can be used correctly or incorrectly, in utterances that are either true or false.

A second difference between natural meaning and non-natural meaning noted by Grice is that one may say that the 'utterer' (the bus conductor or the speaker) means something by the 'utterance' (those three rings of the bell, or 'It is sunny today in Toronto'). Behind the utterance, so to speak, there is an agent who wants to convey some information, or at least to represent herself as conveying some information. There is no such agent in the case of natural meaning. This difference is connected to what I referred to above as the intentional aspect of language use. Both the conductor and the speaker are intentional agents: they produce sounds for a reason, to fulfil a purpose. This is the feature of language that Grice focuses on in order to understand the nature of linguistic meaning better.

Accordingly, Grice proposes that we shed light on what words mean – on what it is for them to mean what they do – by reflecting on what people mean by their words – on what it is for them to mean what they do by their words. According to his analysis, for an agent to mean something non-naturally by an utterance (in Grice's extended sense) and, so, for a speaker to mean something by an utterance (in the usual sense) is for the agent and the speaker to produce the utterance with the intention of bringing about a certain effect on an audience and to intend to do so 'by means of the recognition of the intention' (Grice, 1989, p. 219). The intended effect yields what the agent or the speaker means by her utterance. (We'll see later how this in turn yields the meaning of the sentence uttered.)

Let us first unpack the claim that the intention of producing a certain effect must be 'by means of the recognition of the intention'. To begin with, for an act of meaning to be performed, it is not enough for the agent to intend her utterance to produce some effect – say, to induce some belief in some audience. The agent must also intend the audience to recognize the intention behind the utterance. Thus, to use one of Grice's examples, someone's leaving Jones's handkerchief at the scene of the murder with the intention of inducing the belief that Jones was the murderer is not enough for that agent to mean anything non-naturally by her utterance – that is, in this case, her action; she must have done this also with the intention that her audience recognize the intention behind the utterance. But this additional intention is not yet sufficient to secure non-natural meaning.

Suppose, to use again an example of Grice's, that I want to let Jim know that his wife Catherine and his friend Jules are having an affair. I could induce this belief in Jim either by showing him a photo of Jules displaying 'undue familiarity' with Catherine or by drawing a picture of Jules's behaviour and showing it to

Jim. What is the difference relevant to our enquiry? In the photograph case, Jim's recognition of my intention is irrelevant to the production of the intended effect. Jim could acquire the belief just by finding the photo in his office, where the photo was accidentally dropped. In the drawing case, on the other hand, the recognition makes a difference: if Jim does not recognize my intention, if, say, he thinks that I am just trying to be artistic, the intended effect will not be produced. Thus, for an agent to mean something non-naturally by an utterance, the effect must be intended to be produced by means of the audience's recognizing that the agent intended to produce that effect. The intention must be that the recognition play a role in producing the effect.

Now that we know that for a speaker to mean something by an utterance is for her to produce that utterance with the relevant set of intentions (sometimes called Gricean intentions), we can say in two steps what it is for a sentence (or an expression; for simplicity, I'll stick to sentences) to mean what it does. The meaning of a sentence is to be specified by a statement or a collection of statements about what people mean by utterances of that sentence, which in turn is specified by a statement or collection of statements about what people intend to effect by producing such utterances (bearing in mind that these effects must be intended to be produced by means of the recognition of the intention). But I would be hard pressed to give an example here, for the pressing question at this stage is: of all the intentions that speakers may have, just which intention is relevant to what they mean by their utterances and, hence, to the meaning of the sentences they utter?

Presumably, as noted before, if I utter 'There is a snake!' with the intention of making my addressee leave the room, his leaving the room does not provide the meaning of 'There is a snake!' Or, if I utter 'Move over!' with the intention of annoying my addressee, his getting annoyed does not provide the meaning of 'Move over!'

Grice's answer to the question what intention is relevant to what speakers mean by their utterances is that it is the 'primary' intention, and this intention is the intention that is 'normally' conveyed (or 'normally' intended to be conveyed). I'll comment here on the idea of primary intention and in section 2.5 on the idea of normally conveyed intention.

Given that any utterance may be produced to achieve all kinds of effects that have nothing to do with what speakers mean by that utterance and thus, if Grice is right, with the meaning of the sentence they utter, the only candidate for primary intention seems to be the intention of inducing a belief or conveying some information about the state of mind of the speaker. For instance, if I say 'There is a snake!' in order to induce my addressee to believe that I believe that there is a snake, his acquiring this belief is the primary intended effect; and if I do this in order to make him leave the room, his acting in this way is one of the many possible further intended effects. Or if I say 'Move over!' in order to induce my addressee to believe that I wish him to move over, that is the primary intended effect; and if I do so in order to annoy him, that is one of the many possible further intended effects. The primary intended effect, it seems, is thus to convey the content of the speakers' beliefs or desires. Unfortunately, as we shall soon see, this reveals a shortcoming with Grice's analysis of meaning.

2.4   Assessing the solution

Before examining the shortcomings of Grice's analysis, however, I want to look at its strengths. The major strength, to my mind, is the emphasis on the connection between language and mind. In particular, it is the emphasis on the intentional aspect of language use and how exquisitely this aspect is articulated, by unravelling the special kinds of intentions that capture the states of mind speakers are in (not that they are always actively thinking about these intentions) when they genuinely engage in linguistic behaviour. To repeat, a speech act, like any genuine act, is intentional. But what makes a speech act intentional is more complex than what makes other acts intentional. For it involves an intended meeting of minds, so to speak: the speaker's mind and her audience's. The speaker does not intend just to do something, which is basically to get a message across, but intends to do it in a very special way. This is what many philosophers take a genuine act of meaning to be. But the special nature of the intentions betrays the limitation of the analysis.

Recall once more that Grice's goal is to explain what it is for words to mean what they do by asking first what it is for speakers to mean what they do by their words. Importantly, for them to mean something by their words, they must intend the words they utter to produce a certain effect through the recognition of their intention, an effect that, in turn, is supposed to provide what they mean by the utterance. As I indicated earlier, the only effect that could be associated with the utterance in such a way as to be guaranteed to provide what speakers mean by the utterance, and hence the meaning of the sentence they utter, is that of inducing the belief that the speaker is in the state of mind expressed by the utterance. But this is tantamount to saying that the relevant intended effect is linguistic. And now the question is: what determines the content of the state of mind? We cannot say simply that it is the content of the state of mind expressed by the sentence that is uttered, since we are supposed to be explaining the meaning of that sentence in terms of what speakers mean by utterances of it. We need an account of what sentences mean; and we do not have it.

In light of what I noted in the introductory chapter, this shortcoming should come as no surprise: given how closely the contents of mental states such as intentions are connected to the meanings of the sentences that express them, it is hardly to be expected that the notion of meaning could interestingly be reduced to that of mental content and, thus, that the notion of meaning could be fully explained by appeal to that of intention. If the notion of meaning itself is to be at all illuminated, what we need is an account of what it is for the intention to mean what it does, that is, to have the content it does – an account that does not appeal to something that is already full of meaning or content. I'll say more about this in the next chapter. For now, let us just note that this is not an explanation Grice provides, and his analysis is therefore incomplete. But this is not the only respect in which it is incomplete.

Although the intentional aspect of meaning is nicely elucidated, two other essential ingredients of meaning remain unaccounted for. One has to do with the claim that linguistic expressions, in order to be meaningful, must be governed by standards of correct application. An adequate account of meaning must tell us where these standards come from. To say what it is for words to mean what they do is in part to say what it is for their use to be governed by the standards of correctness they are governed by. Grice is silent about these standards and that is not surprising, as his analysis of meaning relies on the notion of intention, which is itself too closely connected to that of meaning.

The other feature that remains unaccounted for is what I called the novel aspect of language use: the fact that we constantly understand and produce utterances of sentences we have not previously heard or produced. Grice remains silent about this, too, which is also not surprising, as he does not distinguish among types of expressions and says nothing about their structure. Thus he says nothing about how words may be combined in different ways to create novel meaningful utterances.

In short, then, Grice has accounted for only one of the fundamental features of meaning: its intentional aspect.

Of course, nothing he has said precludes there being illuminating things to say about the other features. His analysis is just incomplete. Before turning to ways of completing it, I want to look at a certain manner of distinguishing among kinds of speech acts and the connections among them. This should consolidate our initial understanding of the particular notion of meaning that is the primary object of our study.

2.5   Three kinds of speech acts

Shortly before the publication of Grice's intention-based analysis of meaning, another British philosopher, J. L. Austin, was delivering lectures, eventually published in 1962, that try to sharpen our understanding of 'meaning' – according to him, a 'hopelessly ambiguous or wide word' (Austin, 1962, p. 100) – by focusing on the things we do when we speak and thus, like Grice, by focusing on the connection between meaning and language users. According to Austin, when we utter words, there are several kinds of speech acts we perform or, more accurately, several different descriptions of the act we perform – since there is only one thing we do, which is to issue an utterance. Austin himself refers to different 'aspects' of the 'total' speech act, though his main interest was in the illocutionary kind (soon to be elucidated), and subsequently 'speech act' acquired a more technical meaning, referring usually to that kind (I'll stick here to the non-technical use). The kinds or aspects most important for our purposes are the following three.

When we issue an utterance, we first perform a locutionary act, which Austin describes as the act *of* saying something, that is, of uttering words with a certain literal meaning. For example we utter 'Move over!' with the literal meaning that you move over. At the same time as we perform a locutionary act, we perform an illocutionary act, which Austin describes as the act performed *in* saying something, that is, the act of uttering words with a certain force such as that of a request or that of a recommendation. For example we utter 'Move over!' with the force of asking or advising the audience to move over. Finally, 'normally' we perform a perlocutionary act, which Austin describes as the act performed *by* saying something, that is, the act of achieving some effect. For example by saying 'Move over!' we annoy our audience, we distract it, or we just get it to move over.

There might thus be many perlocutionary effects that we produce by uttering words, some intended, others not. We may also fail to produce the effect we intended to produce, as when I say 'Is there any salt?' with the force of an order, and my audience replies that there is salt but does not pass it to me. Very occasionally, we may produce no perlocutionary effect, as when our utterance is simply ignored (hence my saying above that we 'normally' perform a perlocutionary act). Also, though most often communication will be successful only if the audience is recognizing the three aspects of the speech act the speaker has intended to perform, sometimes the success of a speech act requires that one of the intended perlocutionary effects not be recognized by the audience – as when one of the speaker's intended effects is to deceive her audience.

I suggested in section 2.2 that neither the illocutionary nor the perlocutionary act a speaker performs could provide a path to the meaning of her utterance or, in Austin's terminology, to the locutionary act she has performed. This, in essence, is because any sentence with a given literal meaning can be uttered with all kinds of different forces and to achieve all kinds of perlocutionary effects. Still, it could be said that normally, or typically, a certain kind of grammatical mood, which is part of the literal meaning of a sentence, is used in order to perform a certain kind of illocutionary act. Thus, to mention the most obvious moods, a declarative sentence normally has the force of an assertion, an imperative sentence that of an order, an interrogative sentence that of a question. Moreover, it could be said, following Grice, that there are perlocutionary effects that utterances normally produce and that these are the effects that provide the meanings of the sentences uttered. These effects, as we saw, if they were really to yield the meanings of the sentences without presupposing them (or other things, such as the contents of intentions, which are too closely associated with them), would have to be non-linguistic. So the effects in question could not just be getting an audience to understand the utterances, or to acquire beliefs that the speaker is in the states of mind expressed by the utterances. An example of a perlocutionary effect that might do the trick would be getting the audience to eat their eggplant by uttering 'Eat your eggplant!' However, both attempts – that of linking literal meaning to a 'normal' illocutionary force and that of linking literal meaning to a 'normal' perlocutionary effect (keeping in mind that this must be non-linguistic) – face the same difficulty.

To start with the first attempted link, there is no denying that there is a connection between mood and the idea of an illocutionary force – for example, an imperative labels itself as an order. But the difficulty here is in specifying when the circumstances in which a sentence is uttered are normal or typical, and so when the imperative mood is indeed being used with the force of an order. Is there in fact any interesting way to spell out what makes for normal or typical circumstances? To say that an imperative is used with the force of an order unless the speaker attaches a different force to her utterance, such as that of an assertion or that of a warning, obviously will not do. As for the idea of there being a normal perlocutionary effect that is connected to the literal meaning of a sentence, it faces a similar difficulty: how do we specify, in a non-circular way, the circumstances that must obtain for the expected link between perlocutionary effect and literal meaning to be realized? For instance, how do we specify the circumstances that must obtain for an utterance of 'Eat your eggplant!' to have the 'normal' perlocutionary effect of getting the audience to eat their eggplant? We might try saying that the audience is to perform the action that is described by the utterance, whose literal meaning is that the audience is to eat their eggplant. But this sheds no light on the link between perlocutionary effect and literal meaning, as literal meaning is being invoked in order to specify which perlocutionary effect is normal.

On the basis of considerations such as these, Donald Davidson, a prominent twentieth-century American philosopher of language, concluded that the fact that literal meaning cannot be derived from perlocutionary effect or from illocutionary force is a feature essential to language, a feature that he calls the autonomy of meaning.

2.6   The autonomy of meaning

To say that literal meaning is autonomous is not to deny that every locutionary act is also an illocutionary act and normally a perlocutionary act. Nor is it to deny that a speaker intends every speech act she performs to have a perlocutionary effect, just as she intends to utter words with a certain meaning and with a certain force. But to say that literal meaning is autonomous is to say that the locutionary act comes first in the order of acts that are performed by a speaker, insofar as, again, a sentence with a given literal meaning can be used to perform any number of illocutionary acts and to achieve any number of perlocutionary effects. To be clear, it is not as if the speaker first intends her words to have a certain meaning, then intends them to have a certain force, and then intends them to achieve a certain effect. After all, she does only one thing: produce an utterance. The point is that the meaning her words have is not dependent on their force. More importantly, and perhaps more obviously, this meaning is not dependent on any (non-linguistic) perlocutionary effect the speaker intends to achieve. To put it another way, the illocutionary and perlocutionary acts she performs when she utters words are all performed by means of her performing a locutionary act.

The connections among these acts may be made more conspicuous if we consider them from the point of view of the audience. Usually the locutionary act comes first in the order of understanding. Thus, in most cases, an audience cannot understand what perlocutionary effect a speaker wants to achieve in uttering words unless it understands what the literal meaning of the words is and with what force they are being uttered. Indeed, in most cases it could be said that it is only if the audience gets the intended linguistic effect – gets to understand what state of mind is expressed by the utterance – that it will understand which ulterior non-linguistic effect the speaker wishes to accomplish by means of producing the linguistic effect. However, even if we can sometimes retrieve the meaning of a word by figuring out what non-linguistic effect the speaker intended to achieve with her utterance, it is still not the case that articulating the effect yields the meaning of the word. Thus, to give an example inspired by Davidson, we may understand that Ms Malaprop means *epithet* by 'epitaph' when she says 'That was a nice arrangement of epitaphs', because we understand that she intends to praise the poet who arranged the epithets. Still, praising the poet does not yield the meaning of 'epitaph', even as it is used here to mean *epithet*. One lesson to draw from this is that we must be careful to distinguish between what it takes to communicate and what it takes for words to mean what they do. Although, as we'll see in chapter 5, what makes communication possible and what makes meaning possible may be intimately connected, not everything relevant to communication is relevant to meaning.

What the foregoing suggests is that meaning, to put it shortly, has to come from somewhere else in order for language to be used to achieve the multifarious purposes it can and does achieve. (This is not to deny that minds and intentions are needed, but we need to know more about these intentions.) What in effect has been neglected by focusing on the connection between meaning and language users, instructive though it has been, is the other connection I mentioned in the introduction: the connection between meaning and the extralinguistic reality we talk about when we use language. This is the connection that earlier philosophers of language focused on, and to which I turn in the next chapter.

One other clarificatory note before I proceed. What has become more and more apparent in the foregoing is that the primary object of our study is literal meaning: the meaning attached to the locutionary aspect of a speech act. Thus, when we talk about what a speaker means by her words, we are primarily interested in what she literally means by her words, and not in what she may imply by her words. For instance, if I recommend a student for an academic job by saying that he has excellent handwriting, I may imply that the student is a bad philosopher, but this is not what I literally mean by 'The student has excellent handwriting.' Interestingly, just as literal meaning precedes (in the way described here) force and effect, so, it seems, does it precede implied meaning. My implying that the student is a bad philosopher depends, at least in part, on what I literally mean by 'The student has excellent handwriting.'

References

Austin, J. L. 1962. *How to Do Things with Words*, edited by J. O. Urmson. Harvard University Press.

Davidson, Donald. 2001 [1984]. 'Communication and Convention', in his *Inquiries into Truth and Interpretation*. Oxford University Press, 265–280.

Grice, H. P. 1989 [1957]. 'Meaning', in his *Studies in the Way of Words*. Harvard University Press, 213–223.

Further Readings

On the distinction between natural and non-natural meaning:

Grice, H. P. 1989 [1980]. 'Meaning Revisited', in his *Studies in the Way of Words*. Harvard University Press, 283–303.

On implied meaning:

Grice, H. P. 1989 [1977]. 'Presupposition and Conversational Implicature', in his *Studies in the Way of Words*. Harvard University Press, 269–282.

Important extensions and evaluations of Grice's account of meaning:

Avramides, Anita. 1989. *Meaning and Mind: An Examination of a Gricean Account of Language*. MIT Press.

Neale, Stephen. 1992. 'Paul Grice and the Philosophy of Language'. *Linguistics and Philosophy*, 15(5): 509–559.

Schiffer, Stephen R. 1972. *Meaning*. Oxford University Press.

Strawson, P. F. 2004 [1964]. 'Intention and Convention', in his *Logico-Linguistic Papers*. Routledge, 115–129.

Classical discussions of speech acts:

Austin, J. L. 1961. 'Performative Utterances', in J. O. Urmson and G. J. Warnock (eds), *Philosophical Papers*. Oxford University Press, 220–239.

Searle, John R. 1969. *Speech Acts: An Essay in the Philosophy of Language*. Cambridge University Press.

A recent overview of important developments in speech act theory:

Harris, Daniel W., Daniel Fogal and Matt Moss. 2018. 'Speech Acts: The Contemporary Theoretical Landscape', in Daniel W. Harris, Daniel Fogal and Matt Moss (eds), *New Work on Speech Acts*. Oxford University Press, 1–39.

3

Where Does Meaning Come from?

This chapter starts by addressing head-on the puzzle mentioned in the introduction: what makes it the case that certain signs – sounds or inscriptions – that are produced by human beings are meaningful and capable of being used to communicate many things that could not otherwise be communicated? To put it the way Ludwig Wittgenstein, one of the great philosophers of the twentieth century, once suggested, what must be added to dead signs for them to become alive and thus meaningful? (Wittgenstein himself, as we'll see in chapters 6 and 7, ultimately rejected the question.) As we saw in the previous chapter, their being meaningful may depend on how they are produced, and in particular on their production's being accompanied by certain intentions. But, as we also saw, appealing to intentions does not answer – at least not fully – the question of what must be added; for intentions are themselves full of content, that is to say, full of meaning, and to be told that what must be added to dead signs for them to become meaningful is meaning, though perhaps not false, is rather uninformative. It would be nice to find something to add that is not itself loaded with meaning.

Prima facie at least, there seem to be two possible basic answers to the question what makes words meaningful, and each one falls under a similar conception of meaning (which I shall later call 'the associative conception of meaning'). Words are meaningful either just because they are associated with items inside the minds of speakers or just because they are associated with items outside the minds of speakers.

3.1   Looking for meaning inside the mind

An early proponent of the view that what makes words meaningful is their being associated with items in the minds of speakers was the seventeenth-century British philosopher John Locke, who maintained that words stand for ideas in the minds of those who use them. These ideas, which are, in the first instance, mental images or pictures of some kind, are the 'significations' of words. For instance, the mental picture of a leaf provides the word 'leaf' with its meaning. On the face of it, this is quite a natural answer to give, especially if, like Locke, one thinks that the function of language is to express and communicate one's thoughts, which are themselves composed of ideas. But there are problems with this intuitive answer.

The immediate problem has to do with communication. The ideas that words stand for, which are to be found in speakers' minds, are not accessible to anyone but the speakers who use those words – that is, each speaker has access only to her own ideas. We may then wonder what makes it the case that the idea associated with one word by a speaker is the same as the idea associated with the same word by another speaker, and hence what makes it possible for the speakers to understand each other. The problem, though, is not just that, very probably, different speakers associate different ideas with the same word. The problem does not have to do merely with communication. If an idea could supply a word with meaning, at least we could have meaningful words, even if we might not be able to communicate through them. But can an idea, all by itself, accomplish this meaning-endowing feat?

The fundamental question here is this: what makes it the case that the idea one has in mind is the idea it is, such that it provides the word associated with it the meaning it does? For instance, what makes a mental picture the picture of a leaf rather than the picture of a shape, or of a colour (since presumably the mental picture of a leaf portrays it as having some shape and some colour)? As Wittgenstein, whose example I am borrowing, asked, what makes a picture the picture of pure green rather than the picture of all that is greenish? And what shape must this picture be? Rectangular? Then it might be the picture of a green rectangle. Irregular? Then it might be the picture of irregularity of shape. The fact of the matter is that having a picture in mind might not be sufficient to provide a word with meaning. On the face of it, any picture can be the picture of a variety of things; it is only if the speaker regards it as a picture of a particular kind of thing that the picture in question might be said to provide a word with meaning, which is to say that it might provide a standard one would appeal to in order to assess the applications of the word as correct or incorrect. Needless to say, neither is it necessary to have a picture in mind in order to provide a word with meaning. This is most obviously true of abstract words such as 'wisdom', for which pictures are not even available.

It is important to note that any answer to the question 'Where does meaning come from?' that appeals simply to items in the minds of speakers has to confront this problem: what makes the mental item the item it is, such that it provides the word it is correlated with the meaning it does? This is a problem that all 'mentalist' proposals have to confront, if they are in the business of giving a full answer to the question of what it is for words to have meaning. Central among contemporary views of this sort are those that associate the meanings of expressions with mental 'representations', items in the mind that are supposed to depict or otherwise represent bits of (usually) extra-mental reality. Again, the question arises as to what makes the representation the representation that it is. A possible answer is that the representation is associated with a certain state of the brain that is characterized in non-mental terms. I won't pursue this option here, though I will address it a bit in chapter 6. For now, suffice it to say that the idea of associating a mental item with a state of the brain seems as problematic as the idea of associating an expression with a mental item. Just as we asked what it is about the mental item supposed to be associated with an expression that gives that expression the meaning it has, we may now ask what it is about the brain state supposed to be associated with a mental item that gives that mental item the meaning it has. The other option, if we want to account for the meaning of mental items, is to look for something outside the minds of speakers.

Indeed, the problems outlined here might be taken care of if we knew something about the origins of the mental items, ideas or whatnot that words are supposed to stand for or be correlated with. If, as it may be plausible to surmise, these mental items were themselves caused by items that are public and accessible to all speakers, the same mental items might be associated by different speakers with the same words, as the same external items would cause speakers to have those mental items. Thus, if speakers are caused to have the idea of a leaf by interacting with leaves, chances are that they will be right in understanding each other as meaning *leaf* by 'leaf', even though they might even have different images of leaves in their minds. This additional step – revealing the origins of ideas or mental items that are supposed to give meaning to expressions – would not only explain communication; it would also, crucially, expand the explanation of what makes it the case that words mean what they do, by explaining what makes it the case that the mental items they are associated with are the items they are.

The very crude sketch of this additional step I just gave will be refined in the following chapters. For now, the strong suggestion to be drawn from the foregoing discussion is that, in order to get a satisfactory answer to the question where meaning comes from, we must look outside speakers' minds.

3.2   Looking for meaning outside the mind

An early proponent of the view that at least some meaning comes from outside the mind was the nineteenth-century British philosopher John Stuart Mill. Mill's view that is most often discussed and to some extent still advocated concerns ordinary proper names, that is, expressions that designate definite entities in the world such as people (e.g. 'Emmanuel Macron'), cities (e.g. 'Toronto'), rivers (e.g. 'the Amazon'), mountains (e.g. 'Kilimanjaro'), and the like. Proper names are a good kind of linguistic expression to focus on, especially if we think that the primary function of language is to communicate and the primary function of communication is for us to exchange information about the world around us as we try to convey our various attitudes towards it, what we believe it, suspect it, assume it and so on to be like and what we wish it, hope it, fear it and so on to be like. The link between language use and extralinguistic reality seems to be omnipresent, so it would be nice to understand how this link is established; this should teach us something about meaning. Proper names are interesting, then, for it seems that their connection to entities in the world is immediate; they directly hook onto them, so to speak, they seem to be made just to pick them out, without our otherwise thinking about the entities that are picked out. Very likely, something like this was the intuition that prompted Mill's view, according to which all there is to the meaning of a name is its connection to the entity it designates or refers to – call this entity the referent of the name (actually, 'strictly speaking', according to Mill, proper names have no 'signification'; they only 'denote' objects). However, as you might expect, there are problems with this view. (From now on, unless otherwise indicated, I will use simply 'names' to refer to ordinary proper names.)

Perhaps the most conspicuous worry is this: do we not constantly use, perfectly meaningfully, names that do not have a referent? To take one of the favourite examples of philosophers, 'Pegasus' – the name of a winged horse in Greek mythology – does not refer to any existing entity. As philosophers put it, names such as this are empty. But then, how can they occur in meaningful sentences? This problem is a variation on another one, which the German philosopher Gottlob Frege, one of the founders of analytic philosophy, was to address head-on. Frege's initial problem is often referred to as 'Frege's puzzle'.

3.3   Frege's puzzle

The problem with Mill's view is not just that names that lack a referent can be used meaningfully; the problem is also that different names are sometimes used to refer to the same entity. For example, both 'Hesperus' (the name given the planet Venus when seen in the evening) and 'Phosphorus' (the name given the planet Venus when seen in the morning) are used to refer to the same planet, Venus. Consider then these identity statements: 'Hesperus is Hesperus' and 'Hesperus is Phosphorus.' What is the difference between the two? The first one is trivially true. But the second one could be – indeed, once was – news. It was an empirical discovery that Hesperus is Phosphorus. But if all there were to the meaning of a name were its referent, no one who understood the statement 'Hesperus is Phosphorus' could ever have failed to know that the statement is true. Understanding it, knowing its meaning, would be tantamount to knowing that the names have the same referent. But one can understand a true identity statement without knowing that its names co-refer. Again, unlike the statement 'Hesperus is Hesperus', the statement 'Hesperus is Phosphorus' can be informative. As Frege put it, the two statements have different cognitive values. How can this be?

Perhaps the key to a solution here is to acknowledge that, when we are told 'Hesperus is Phosphorus', we learn something not just about language – namely that the two names are used to refer to the same object – but about the world – namely that a certain heavenly body seen in the evening is the same as a certain heavenly body seen in the morning. We learn that it is the same object that is causing us to have two different visual experiences, the same object that is 'presented' or 'given' to us in two different ways. Accordingly, Frege's answer to the question why the two identity statements have different cognitive values and how a true identity statement can be informative is that the names, here 'Hesperus' and 'Phosphorus', though they have the same referent, the planet Venus, have different 'senses', as he calls them – perhaps the senses provided respectively by the definite descriptions 'the evening star' and 'the morning star'. (Definite descriptions are introduced by the definite article 'the' and, like names, are used to pick out definite entities, in contrast with indefinite descriptions such as 'a large star', which apply to more than one entity.) This is to say that, according to Frege, there is more to the meaning of a name than its referent.

Frege then defines the sense of a name as that in which the 'mode of presentation' of its referent is contained. To make the idea of mode of presentation a little more intelligible, it might help to recognize something that may go against the intuition I earlier attributed to Mill. When we use a name to talk about an object, we often think of the object not just directly, as it were, but under some guise or aspect, under some particular description. Thus we may think of the sense of a name as a way of thinking about, or apprehending, the object it refers to. As Frege puts it, a sense 'illuminates' a single aspect of the object, which may be referred to by different names with different senses, each illuminating a different aspect. Importantly, according to Frege, senses are objective, that is, as he spells it out, known by anyone who is familiar with the language. He makes a point of contrasting senses with 'conceptions' – any images or ideas one may associate with names – which are subjective. Thus, to use Frege's example, a painter, a rider, and a zoologist may associate different conceptions with the name of a horse such as 'Bucephalus', but (ideally: see next paragraph) not different senses. This makes it obvious how significantly Frege's account differs from Locke's: there meanings stem from psychological states, which is precisely what Frege wanted to avoid, in part for fear of making meaning subjective.

The objectivity of senses explains the success of communication, but we may still wonder what exactly these senses are and what makes their objectivity possible. Frege himself concedes that different speakers may associate different descriptions with the same name. He gives the example of 'Aristotle', which some speakers may associate with 'the pupil of Plato and teacher of Alexander the Great' and others with 'the teacher of Alexander the Great who was born in Stagira'. Frege thinks that such 'variations of sense' are acceptable so long as the referent of the name remains the same. The thought here presumably is that speakers are still talking about the same thing. But just how can they? If speakers are to communicate with one another while using the name 'Aristotle', that is, if they are to know that they are talking about the same entity, they must know which definite description each speaker associates with 'Aristotle', and, if these descriptions vary from one speaker to the next, they must know that their descriptions are co-referential, that is, they all refer to the same person, Aristotle. If they do not need this knowledge, this shows that the descriptions were not necessary after all to provide the name with meaning. Moreover, looking at matters from the first-person point of view, insofar as we do associate names with definite descriptions when we use them, it is unlikely that we associate the same description with the same name on every occasion of use.

These worries are connected to another pressing question: how do speakers get to attach one or the other description to a name? Moreover, and perhaps even more pressingly, how does the description itself get to have the meaning it does? The first question is especially pressing if we keep in mind that empty names can still have a sense. This seems to solve the problem of how they can be used meaningfully, but in their case there are no objects that present themselves in certain ways. Where, then, do these senses come from? How do we get hold of them? And even when a name is not empty and there is an object that it refers to, the object can present itself in any number of ways. How do we settle on the presentation, and hence description, that will provide the sense of the name and allow for communication?

It is unclear what Frege's answers to those questions might be. But he did eventually suggest that senses are to be found neither in the external world nor in the mind, but in a third, abstract realm. This may help us to explain how descriptions get to mean what they do. In particular, it may help us to explain how empty names can be meaningful, even though no objects in the world are presented to us in the way indicated by the descriptions. Descriptions are composed of predicates, such as 'is a pupil'. And, according to Frege, every significant constituent of a sentence has a sense. Thus predicates, too, have a sense. The sense of a predicate is the mode of presentation of its referent, which Frege calls a function, a kind of abstract entity. Examples are concepts such as the concept of being green, and relations such as the relation of being larger than. We still have to explain, however, how we get hold of those senses, how particular predicates get to be connected with the particular senses that allegedly give them the meaning they have, and how they get to be connected to items in the world. We may indeed wonder why the detour via abstract senses is needed – why not say that items in the world directly provide our words with the meaning they have? We'll return to this question in the next chapter. For now, we must examine – besides the informativeness of some true identity statements and the meaningfulness of empty names – another puzzling linguistic fact that Frege thinks his distinction between sense and referent can solve.

3.4   Frege's other puzzle

To introduce this puzzle, we must first finish describing Frege's distinction between sense and referent. As I said earlier, according to Frege, every significant constituent of a sentence has a sense. A sentence with a senseless constituent is itself senseless, that is, meaningless. Indeed, the sense of a sentence depends on the senses of its constituents. What is the sense of a sentence (sticking here, as Frege does, to declarative sentences of the subject–predicate form)? It is what Frege calls a thought, that is, an objective content, which, like any sense, is supposed to exist independently of any speaker and can be shared by many speakers. Now, every significant constituent of a sentence (normally) also has a referent. So, too, does the sentence itself. We know that the referent of a name is a definite entity and the referent of a predicate is something abstract, which Frege thinks of as a function that is supposed to take an object as input and yield a truth value (true or false) as output. For example, the referent of the predicate 'is Canadian', if it takes the object Justin Trudeau as input, yields the value true. 'Justin Trudeau is Canadian' is a true sentence. According to Frege, then, the referent of a declarative sentence is its truth value. As he puts it, it is either the true, the circumstance that it is true, or the false, the circumstance that it is false. This entails that all true sentences have the same referent and all false sentences have the same referent, which is rather perplexing. After all, all true sentences are not about the same event or state of affairs, and all false sentences are not about the denial of the same event or state of affairs. How, then, can all true sentences have the same referent and all false sentences have the same referent?

Part of Frege's explanation is that, when considering declarative sentences, we are often concerned with the referents of their constituents, and this is because we are concerned with the truth value of declarative sentences. All this indicates that the referent of a declarative sentence is its truth value. But what are we to make of this? To be sure, to figure out the truth value of a sentence, if we follow Frege, we have to ensure that its constituents have referents, but we also need to figure out whether the predicate expression does apply to the referent of the name, whether, say, 'Canadian' applies to Justin Trudeau. This sounds as if we need to figure out whether something in the world is the case, which in turn suggests that the referent of a declarative sentence is something more specific than its truth value. But there is another consideration that might help partly to explain what Frege had in mind when he concluded that the referents of declarative sentences are either the true or the false. Frege also thinks of these referents as objects, though obviously of a different kind from ordinary objects. The thought here is that sentences, like names, but unlike predicates, are complete expressions, and complete expressions designate objects. Though Frege himself does not say so, it may help to understand this a bit if we think of names and sentences as being able by themselves to capture a particular thing in the world or to say something about the world, whereas a predicate needs something to be added to it in order to do that. Thus it could be said that 'Justin Trudeau', all by itself, picks out a person. 'Justin Trudeau is Canadian', all by itself, states something true about the world. But 'is Canadian', all by itself, just refers to something abstract and needs to be attached to a name to say something about the world.

Recall now that Frege thinks of the sense of a name as the mode of presentation of an object; it provides, as it were, a way to keep track of an object, or a way to reach it. We can think of the senses of true sentences in the same way. They all are ways of keeping track of, or reaching, or thinking about, or describing what is true. And the senses of false sentences are, all, ways of keeping track of, or reaching, or thinking about, or describing what is false. This at least spares us the difficulty of saying what the referents of false sentences are. It also spares us the difficulty of saying just how much of the world or just what part of it must be included in the referent of a true sentence.

Now, Frege maintains that, just as the sense of a sentence depends on the senses of its constituents, so the referent of a sentence depends on the referents of its constituents, which, as suggested earlier, is plausible enough. Perhaps less plausibly, he takes this claim to entail that, just as a sentence that contains a constituent without a sense has itself no sense, so a sentence that contains a constituent without a referent has itself no referent, that is, no truth value. This is in fact consistent with Frege's claim that the referent of a predicate is a function. A function needs an input – an object – in order to yield an output – a truth value; so, if there is no input, there is no output. Still, the claim that sentences that contain constituents without a referent have no truth value may strike us as less plausible; for, prima facie at least, we may think that such sentences are false, as there is nothing in the world that they are about. For instance, the sentence 'Louis XIII woke up early this morning' is false, since such a person no longer exists. To say instead that it is neither true nor false may appear to some as rather puzzling, as we shall soon see. But first we must examine the other puzzle the present section is about. This puzzle is generated by the Fregean tenets that the referent of a sentence depends on the referents of its constituents and that the referent of a sentence is its truth value. Frege thinks that an elaboration of his distinction between sense and referent can solve it.

Consider the following two sentences – an example from another famous twentieth-century American philosopher, W. V. O. Quine: 'The man in the brown hat is a spy' and 'Ortcutt is a spy.' And assume that the definite description 'the man in the brown hat' and the name 'Ortcutt' refer to the same person. For Frege, whether a sentence of this form is true or false depends in part on whether the name or the definite description picks out a definite entity and in part on whether the predicate applies to that entity. Since here the two expressions, 'Ortcutt' and 'the man in the brown hat', are co-referring, the two sentences have the same truth value. Whatever applies to the person referred to by the name 'Ortcutt' applies as well to the person referred to by the definite description 'the man in the brown hat'. In other words, we do not change the truth value of the sentence if we substitute one expression for the other. Now consider the following report: 'Ralph believes that the man in the brown hat is a spy'; and assume that the report is true. Can we substitute 'Ortcutt' here for 'the man in the brown hat' without running the risk of changing the truth value of the report? Suppose

Ralph does not know that the man in the brown hat is Ortcutt. If so, he may not believe that Ortcutt is a spy. The sentence 'Ralph believes that Ortcutt is a spy' may be false. But the truth value of a sentence depends on the referents of its constituents, and the referents are the same in both sentences. How, then, could the two reports have different truth values?

The key for Frege to solve the puzzle is to recognize that the truth value of the that-clause – the clause opened by 'that' – is in fact irrelevant to the truth value of the whole sentence or report. That Ralph has the belief he has is true or false independently of whether his belief is itself true or false. But then the referent of the that-clause cannot be a truth value, Frege's reasoning goes. If it were a truth value, then the truth value of the report would depend in part upon the truth value of the that-clause. What, then, is the referent? According to Frege, it is a thought – that is, the sense that the sentence has ordinarily, which he calls its 'customary' sense. Thus the customary sense becomes the 'indirect' referent. But then, what is the sense of the that-clause? It is what Frege calls its 'indirect' sense, which is to say, in our example, not the sense of the expression 'Ortcutt is a spy' but the sense of the expression 'the thought that Ortcutt is a spy'. In short, in so-called indirect discourse, when the sayings or attitudes of someone are being reported, the expressions in the that-clause have an indirect referent and an indirect sense. The referent of the that-clause is not a truth value but a thought (its customary sense), and the sense of the that-clause is not its customary sense but its indirect sense.

This solution is pretty ingenious, indeed, intuitive, insofar as we do think that when we report, say, someone's belief, the focus is on the content of the belief, not on its truth value. We are reporting a thought, a state of mind, the sense of someone's words, not the event or the state of affairs that the state of mind or words are about – which is not to deny that they are about some external, non-mental event or state of affairs. But the solution is also rather cumbersome, indeed, unintuitive, insofar as it is hard to accept that the senses of the words in the that-clause are different from the ordinary senses of the same words; what could those senses be? The problem becomes even more urgent if we reflect on the fact that reports can be iterated or nested. Thus one could report 'Julie believes that Ralph believes that the man in a brown hat is a spy.' Presumably, following Frege, the sense of the that-clause 'the man in the brown hat is a spy' is different here from the sense it has in the report 'Ralph believes that the man in a brown hat is a spy.' Could we account for these new senses in a systematic way? And, if not, how could we communicate through them?

3.5 Russell's solution to Frege's puzzles

The British philosopher Bertrand Russell, another founder of analytic philosophy, proposed a solution that is altogether different from Frege's. You will have noticed that, in the previous example, I started using not just ordinary proper names but definite descriptions. As we know, expressions of both kinds are used to pick out definite entities (Frege in fact called all such expressions proper names). Nowadays expressions that purport to pick out definite entities are usually referred to as singular terms, to be distinguished from predicates or general terms, which purport to apply to sets of entities. In the essay in which his most forceful criticism of Frege occurs, Russell discusses what he called 'denoting phrases': expressions such as 'a woman', 'all people', 'the present king of France', 'the present king of England'. Russell could not make sense of Frege's senses. According to him, a name is meaningful if it actually refers to, or 'denotes' (Russell's word) something. The thing it denotes, or picks out, or stands for (all these words are equivalent here) is the meaning of the name; so all there is to the meaning of a name is its denotation or referent. If a putative name lacks a denotation or a referent, then either it is meaningless (and all sentences containing it are meaningless) or it is not a genuine name; strange as this may sound, it only appears to be a name (this will become clear later, when we consider 'Apollo'). This view of names is actually similar to Mill's and will eventually lead Russell to say that the only real names are demonstrative expressions like 'this' and 'that', which stand for things with which we are acquainted – that is, things that are given to the mind in a direct, unmediated way, such as the data or impressions of our senses, and whose existence we therefore could not doubt. I won't pursue this disconcerting line of thought here. What we want to know at this stage is how Russell solves Frege's puzzles, starting with the second one.

According to Russell, denoting phrases do not have meaning in isolation, but they do contribute to the meaning of the sentences in which they occur. Once properly analysed in the context of a sentence, the denoting phrases disappear, that is, there is no constituent in the analysed form that corresponds to the denoting phrase in the unanalysed sentence at all. Russell focuses on definite descriptions, which he finds to be 'the most interesting and difficult of denoting phrases' (Russell, 1905, p. 481). Take one of Russell's examples of a definite description, 'the author of *Waverley*'. According to Russell, it has meaning only in the context of a sentence. So, take the sentence 'Scott is the author of *Waverley*.' This sentence's meaning, for Russell, is really the meaning of the sentence 'There is one and only one entity who wrote *Waverley*, and Scott was identical with that one.' In the analysis, the unique existence of some entity or other is asserted, and then something is said about it. But the definite description has disappeared! This magic trick is what enables Russell to solve Frege's second puzzle.

Consider the following report: 'George IV wondered whether the author of *Waverley* was Scott.' Why can we not substitute 'Scott' for 'the author of *Waverley*' in that sentence? To be sure, we do not want to make this substitution – as Russell says, George IV did not wonder whether Scott was Scott! The reason why we cannot substitute is not, as Frege would have it, that expressions in the that-clause do not have their ordinary sense; it is rather that 'the author of *Waverley*' does not have any meaning on its own. It has meaning only in the context of a sentence. Accordingly, it should be contextually analysed, as follows: 'George IV wondered whether there is one and only one entity who wrote *Waverley* and Scott was identical with that one.' The denoting phrase – 'the author of *Waverley*' – has disappeared. So there is no longer anything for which we could substitute 'Scott'. (Let us assume, as Russell does here, that 'Scott' is a real name, whose meaning is its denotation. As we'll soon see, even at this stage, Russell is not always able to treat ordinary proper names as real names.) To go back to the example I used while discussing Frege's solution: 'Ralph believes that the man in the brown hat is a spy.' Why can we not substitute 'Ortcutt' for 'the man in the brown hat'? It is because, according to Russell, 'the man in the brown hat' has no meaning on its own. Again, it should be analysed contextually, as follows: 'Ralph believes that there is one and only one entity who wears the brown hat and that entity is a spy.'

As for Frege's first puzzle, as just hinted, Russell will not be able to solve it unless he replaces 'Hesperus' and 'Phosphorus' with definite descriptions, say, 'the evening star' and 'the morning star'. Then he can analyse the identity statement 'Hesperus is Phosphorus' as follows: 'There is one and only one thing x that is an evening star, and there is one and only one thing y that is a morning star, and x is y.' In order to understand the identity statement, we do not have to know that the two names co-refer – their referent is not their meaning.

And so the statement can be informative. (Empty names can be treated similarly, by replacing the name with a definite description and analysing it contextually.)

Are Russell's solutions to Frege's puzzles more convincing than Frege's? On the one hand, the contextual analyses Russell recommends may strike us as not doing justice to our understanding of how ordinary language functions. In particular, as has often been remarked, we may think not that definite descriptions are used to assert the unique existence of definite entities about which something can then be said, but rather that the unique existence of such entities is presupposed. On the other hand, Russell's solutions may be tempting insofar as they do not postulate mysterious 'indirect' senses, or even any senses at all, which are themselves rather mysterious. But recall that senses were needed for us to account for the meaning of definite descriptions. For it was all very well to say that ordinary proper names really are disguised definite descriptions; we then had to confront the question, whence the meaning of the descriptions? Even if we forgot about senses, insofar as they are conceived of as abstract entities, and we decided that meaning comes from the objects that descriptions are about and that are presented to us in certain ways, there still would be the crucial questions of how those connections are established, how we get hold of them, and which descriptions are meaning-giving. Of course, Russell has to confront the same questions. First, just what provides meaning to the predicates that definite descriptions are made of? Russell suggested that predicates are connected to qualities – for example 'is white' is connected to the quality of whiteness – or relations – for example 'is to the left of' is connected to the relation of being to the left of. But how are these connections established? Moreover, again, which descriptions are the meaning-giving ones and how do they get attached to particular names?

So far we have examined the puzzles that Frege's distinction between sense and referent is supposed to address. We now examine two related puzzles that Russell introduced and took his contextual analysis to contribute to solving.

3.6   Russell's puzzles

Recall that, according to Frege, if a sentence has a constituent that lacks a referent, the sentence itself has no referent, that is, no truth value. This bothered Russell very much, as he thought that it forces us to say that a negative existential statement such as 'Apollo does not exist' is neither true nor false, when it is tempting to say that it is plainly true. Equally problematic are disjunctive sentences such as 'Either the present king of France is bald or the present king of France is not bald', which is also plainly true, according to Russell anyway. But how can this be? Aren't 'The present king of France is bald' and 'The present king of France is not bald' both false? But, for the whole disjunctive sentence to be true, one of the disjuncts has to be true. Russell proposes to solve the problem in the following way.

His answer is that the sentence 'The present king of France is not bald' is ambiguous. Denoting phrases may have what he calls either a 'primary occurrence' or a 'secondary occurrence'. For instance, 'The present king of France' in the sentence 'The present king of France is not bald' has either a primary occurrence or a secondary occurrence. In the former case the sentence is analysed as 'There is an entity that is now king of France and is not bald'; the entity allegedly denoted by the denoting phrase 'the present king of France' is being posited, so to speak – hence presumably Russell's calling the occurrence of the denoting phrase primary. But 'The present king of France' in the sentence 'The present king of France is not bald' can also have a secondary occurrence, in which case it is analysed as 'It is false that there is an entity that is now king of France and is bald.' So analysed, this disjunct is true, and the law of excluded middle – according to which, for every declarative sentence, either that sentence or its negation is true – is respected. For 'The present king of France' has (i) a primary occurrence in 'The present king of France is bald' – and hence the sentence is false: it is false that there is an entity that is now king of France and is bald – and (ii) a secondary occurrence in 'The present king of France is not bald' – and hence the sentence is true: it is true that it is false that there is an entity that is now king of France and is bald.

We can solve the problem of negative existential sentences in a similar way. How can 'Apollo does not exist' have a truth value? Here we have to supply a definite description for 'Apollo' – which, as Russell remarks, clearly is not a genuine name, since it has no denotation (if it did, we would be saying that Apollo, who exists, does not exist, in other words we would be infringing the law of contradiction). Let us, following Russell, associate 'the sun god' with 'Apollo'. Then we can analyse the sentence as follows (again, using the distinction between secondary and primary occurrences and, here, the secondary occurrence): 'It is false that there is one and only one entity that is a sun god', which is a true sentence. We can thus understand how 'Apollo does not exist' is true.

As for Frege's solution to these puzzles, strictly speaking, there is none. All that Frege can do is lament the imperfections of ordinary languages and propose a semi-mathematical treatment that postulates the null class as the denotation or referent of empty names, a procedure Russell rightly took to be artificial.

3.7   A hopeless enterprise?

At this stage, you may well lament with Frege that ordinary languages are hopelessly imperfect, and conclude that the project of giving a complete and systematic account of linguistic meaning is hopelessly ambitious. Too many intricacies, too many details. But we have barely scratched the surface of what can be done! And some progress has been made: Frege's and Russell's accounts at least make it possible to see how we can understand new sentences and how expressions can be governed by standards of correct application. Expressions can be so governed, Frege and Russell hold, because they are associated with particular entities that provide the standards that determine whether the expressions have been applied correctly or not. Thus the entity giving the meaning of 'green' provides the standard that determines whether I apply 'green' correctly when I say 'Emeralds are green' and whether I apply it incorrectly when I say 'The sky is green.' And we understand new sentences in part because they are composed of expressions whose meaning we already understand. Thus their accounts may be seen as a first step towards fulfilling two of the conditions on an acceptable account of meaning – namely, as I put it in the previous chapter, that it explain, or at least make room for, the novel and standard-governed aspects of meaning. But Frege's and Russell's accounts fail to account for the third aspect I mentioned, which I called the intentional aspect: that which distinguishes genuine linguistic behaviour from automatic behaviour. This failure should come as no surprise since, at least in the texts I have discussed, their focus is on the question what kind of items may provide expressions with meaning, and not, as we have seen repeatedly, on the question how particular expressions get to be connected to particular items. Presumably, shedding light on the intelligent aspect of language use requires addressing the latter question.

Furthermore, studying Frege and Russell helps us to appreciate the complexities of the issues involved, indeed, the scope and the depth of these complexities, as we acknowledge the multifarious and marvellous feats the use of language can achieve. And, noticeably, the difficulties we have encountered have arisen when examining what seems to be the most basic, straightforward uses of language: describing states of affairs or reporting states of mind. Studying Frege and Russell also introduces further constraints that any acceptable account of meaning should strive to meet. An account of meaning that leaves it mysterious how true identity statements can be informative, how empty names can be meaningful, why we cannot substitute co-referring expressions in indirect contexts on pain of changing their truth value, and, perhaps, how every declarative sentence can have a truth value does not seem to be an acceptable account.

We started discussing Frege's view because of its suggestion that we look outside the mind in our search for the sources of meaning. In particular, with his claim that the senses of names contain ways in which external objects are presented to us, Frege suggested that we look at the world around us and at the connection between objects in the world and the meanings of the words we use to talk about them. But it is not obvious that he has done that in the end. (Indeed, as we'll see in the next chapter, he has even been accused of never having left the mind.) It remains very unclear how the objects referred to by our words play a role in determining their meaning. However, if they do play such a role, and if we are to get clear about this, we need to get clear about how the relations between words and what they refer or apply to – bits of extralinguistic reality – are established. We need to scrutinize the relation of reference. This is what we do in the next chapter, at last really leaving the mind for a while.

References

Frege, Gottlob. 1997 [1892]. 'On *Sinn* and *Bedeutung*', translated by Max Black, in Michael Beaney (ed.), *The Frege Reader*. Blackwell, 151–171. [Note: earlier English translations of this paper rendered its title 'On Sense and Reference'. Beaney has chosen to retain the original German terms.]

Locke, John. 1975 [1690]. 'Book III'. *An Essay Concerning Human Understanding*, edited by Peter Nidditch. Oxford University Press.

Mill, John Stuart. 2011 [1843]. 'Of Names', in his *A System of Logic, Ratiocinative and Inductive*. Cambridge University Press, 27–58.

Russell, Bertrand. 1995. 'On Denoting'. *Mind*, 14(56): 479–493.

Wittgenstein, Ludwig. 2009 [1953]. *Philosophical Investigations* (4th edn), edited by P. M. S. Hacker and Joachim Schulte, translated by G. E. M. Anscombe, P. M. S. Hacker and Joachim Schulte. Wiley Blackwell.

Further Readings

On Frege's account of meaning:

Frege, Gottlob. 1997 [1891]. 'Function and Concept', translated by Peter Geach, in Michael Beaney (ed.), *The Frege Reader*. Blackwell, 130–148.

Frege, Gottlob. 1997 [1892]. 'On Concept and Object', translated by Peter Geach, in Michael Beaney (ed.), *The Frege Reader*. Blackwell, 181–193.

Frege, Gottlob. 1997 [1918]. 'Thought', translated by Peter Geach and R. H. Stoothoff, in Michael Beaney (ed.), *The Frege Reader*. Blackwell, 325–345.

An introduction to Frege's work:

Weiner, Joan. 2005. *Frege Explained: From Arithmetic to Analytic Philosophy*. Open Court.

A more accessible introduction to Russell's account of definite descriptions:

Russell, Bertrand. 2022 [1919]. 'Descriptions', in his *Introduction to Mathematical Philosophy*. Routledge, 159–171.

Two influential responses to Russell's account of definite descriptions:

Strawson, P. F. 2004 [1950]. 'On Referring', in his *Logico-Linguistic Papers*. Routledge, 1–20.
Donnellan, Keith S. 1966. 'Reference and Definite Descriptions'. *Philosophical Review*, 75(3): 281–304.

A book-length expansion of Russell's approach to definite descriptions:

Neale, Stephen. 1993. *Descriptions*. MIT Press.

Accounts that suggest that the meanings of our words are in some way fixed by their relation to mental representations, each defending a different version of mentalism:

Fodor, Jerry. 1987. *Psychosemantics: The Problem of Meaning in the Philosophy of Mind*. MIT Press.
Laurence, Stephen. 1996. 'A Chomskian Alternative to Convention-Based Semantics'. *Mind*, 105(418): 269–301.
Pietroski, Paul M. 2018. *Conjoining Meanings: Semantics without Truth Values*. Oxford University Press.

4

Meaning and Reference

This chapter starts to address the crucial question left unanswered by Frege and Russell: how does the connection between words and their referents get established? Let us again focus on ordinary proper names to begin with (again, 'names' for short, in what follows). We saw that, though they attempt to solve in quite different ways the puzzles they introduce, Frege (at least on the orthodox interpretation) and Russell both maintain that names are disguised or abbreviated definite descriptions and their senses or meanings are provided by the definite descriptions speakers associate with them (notwithstanding their disagreement as to how definite descriptions themselves function). It might then be said that a name is connected to its referent, that is, the object it designates, in virtue of the definite description associated with it, which is uniquely satisfied by the object. We saw that, if we want a full answer to the question what it is for a name to mean what it does, we need to say something about the meaning of the words used in the definite description associated with it. But even leaving this problem aside, this classical descriptivist view ultimately does not answer the question how the connection between a name and its referent is established; for, as we saw in the previous chapter, the question of which definite description is relevant to the meaning of the name or how it gets selected does remain, along with the attendant question of how people communicate when they use names with which they associate different definite descriptions. A further problem I have not mentioned so far is that, if the definite description one associates with a name turns out not to be satisfied by the object allegedly referred to by the name, it follows that one was actually never using that name to talk about that object. For instance, one never used the name 'Aristotle' to talk about Aristotle if it turns out that he was never taught by Plato and if the only definite description one associates with 'Aristotle' is 'the Stagira-born pupil of Plato'. But surely one did use the name 'Aristotle' to talk about Aristotle! Indeed, contra those who believe that the description gives the meaning of the name, it is not true by definition that Aristotle was the Stagira-born pupil of Plato. A different version of the descriptivist theory of names, known as the cluster theory of names, was introduced to address these problems.

4.1   The cluster theory of names

This view was first suggested by Wittgenstein and then more systematically developed and defended by the American philosopher John Searle in the late 1950s. Searle acknowledged the aforementioned problems, but did not want to relinquish the claim that names have senses or meanings ('sense' and 'meaning' are used here interchangeably – there is no question for Searle of a Fregean third realm of senses), for doing so generates its own problems or puzzles, which we discussed in the previous chapter. Instead, Searle introduced a new version of descriptivism, which differs from the classical version in two important respects. First, that in virtue of which a name can be used to pick out a definite object is not a single definite description associated with that name. Rather it is a set or cluster of definite descriptions, many but not necessarily all of which apply to (i.e. are true of) the object picked out by the name. It is not specified, though, which descriptions in particular do apply or which particular descriptions any given speaker associates with a given name. For example, 'Aristotle' as commonly used in a community may be associated with descriptions such as 'the Greek philosopher born in Stagira', 'the most famous pupil of Plato', 'the author of the *Nicomachean Ethics*', and so on, some of which could turn out to be false of Aristotle and only some of which need to be associated with the name by anyone who uses it, though not necessarily the same ones by every speaker. Second, Searle makes it sound as if the definite descriptions associated with a name do not define it. As he himself puts it, when we use a proper name, we do not 'assert or specify' any characteristics of the object referred to by the name. Rather we 'presuppose' that the object has certain characteristics. Thus, according to Searle, when we use the name 'Aristotle' to refer to Aristotle, we presuppose that certain definite descriptions do apply to Aristotle, that Aristotle has certain 'unique characteristics', but it remains unspecified which characteristics are presupposed.

How is the cluster theory an improvement on the classical theory?

Searle himself believed that his theory better captures the unique function of names, a function that, as he emphasized, is simply to refer to or pick out an object, not to describe it, which is the function of definite descriptions. Furthermore, the theory avoids the problem the classical descriptivist has of determining which particular description is to be associated with a given name. Relatedly, it makes it much easier than it is for classical descriptivism to explain how people communicate when they use names, as it is much more likely that there will be overlaps among the sets of descriptions interlocutors associate with a name than that there will be coincidences between the one and only description they happen to associate with it. Finally, Searle's theory does not have the unfortunate consequence that it is true by definition that a given description applies to an object. It might turn out to be false that Aristotle was the Stagira-born pupil of Plato; even so, we could still use 'Aristotle' to talk about Aristotle, so long as other definite descriptions associated with the name applied to Aristotle. However, according to Searle, we could not talk about Aristotle if it turned out that *none* of the definite descriptions we commonly presuppose when we use 'Aristotle' applies to Aristotle. It is necessary, Searle insists, that some of these descriptions apply to Aristotle. Thus, Searle makes it sound as if descriptions are defining after all; it is just that the name now seems to be defined by a cluster of descriptions rather than just one. Note, moreover, that Searle has nothing to say about the meaning of the descriptions themselves. In the end, even though his cluster theory improves on the classical descriptivist theory in some respects, it remains vulnerable to some of the same objections. I further examine criticisms of descriptivism in the next section. After that, I'll examine an alternative answer to the question how the connection between name and object is set up.

4.2   Criticizing descriptivism

The most famous critic of descriptivism is the American philosopher Saul Kripke, who in the early 1970s developed, along with his critique, an alternative view of how names refer – all this in a book that was to revolutionize philosophy of language (not to mention metaphysics). For the book was one of the first truly to 'externalize' meaning, that is, to scrutinize the contribution made by the external world to determining what words mean and thus to making it possible for words to have meaning. Kripke presented a battery of arguments against the cluster theory. I'll focus on the three I take to be the most important.

Before presenting the first argument, I should mention a thesis famously advanced by Kripke concerning names. This is the thesis, intuitive according to him, that names are 'rigid designators'. A rigid designator is an expression that designates or refers to the same object in all possible worlds in which the object exists. To clarify, when we talk about 'possible worlds' as Kripke understands them, we are not talking about fanciful science fiction worlds, but simply about different ways in which our world, the actual one, might be or might have been. We are talking about situations that might, contrary to fact, obtain or have obtained. The question is what a name would refer to if, contrary to fact, the object it is used in our language to refer to had different properties from those it has in the actual world. (The claim is not about what names may refer to for the inhabitants of those other possible worlds, which speak languages different from ours.) And Kripke's answer is that it would refer to the same object as it does in our world. Thus, to say that 'Aristotle' is a rigid designator is to say that 'Aristotle' refers to Aristotle in every possible world, including one in which Aristotle was a gardener rather than a philosopher. Definite descriptions, on the other hand, are not rigid designators (at least not normally). The definite description 'the US president in 2024' refers to Joe Biden in the actual world, that is, in our world, but when we talk about another possible world it might refer to Donald Trump. Someone other than Joe Biden could have been the US president in 2024. However, only Joe Biden could have been Joe Biden – as Kripke would put it, in an attempt to capture the intuition behind the claim that names are rigid designators. I now turn to Kripke's first argument against the cluster theory.

According to Kripke (1980, p. 74), it is simply not necessarily true, 'in any intuitive sense of necessity', that the object referred to by a name has any given set of characteristics – in other words, that it has any of the properties commonly attributed to that object. For instance, it is simply not necessarily true that Aristotle was the pupil of Plato and was born in Stagira, that he wrote the *Nicomachean Ethics*, that he was the philosopher who taught Alexander the Great . . . All these properties are only contingently true of Aristotle; they might not have been possessed by him. Aristotle might never have pursued philosophy and might have become a gardener instead. Crucially, we would still be talking about the same person, Aristotle, when we use 'Aristotle'. We would just have a host of false beliefs about him. Searle was obviously right in rejecting classical descriptivism, which seems committed to saying that the one definite description associated with a name necessarily applies to the referent of the name. But Searle's cluster theory turns out to be no improvement on this descriptivism. What is true of one definite description associated with a name, namely that it does not necessarily apply to the referent of the name, is true of a set of definite descriptions, no matter how deeply entrenched they might be.

According to Kripke's second argument, it is not *necessary* to associate *any* definite description with a name in order to succeed in referring to an object by using that name. For instance, to use Kripke's examples, many speakers do not associate a definite description with the name 'Cicero'; they associate only an indefinite description, such as 'a famous Roman orator'. Likewise, they associate only an indefinite description with the name 'Feynman': 'a famous physicist'. Speaking for myself, this is certainly the only description I associate with the name; this is all I know about Feynman (indeed, I learned this from Kripke). But I can imagine myself, even with only this limited knowledge, conversing about Feynman, asking questions and then making comments about him, in short, succeeding in referring to that one person by using the name.

According to Kripke's third argument, it may not even be *sufficient* to associate a definite description with a name in order to succeed in referring to an object by using that name. Kripke presents us with a fanciful scenario in which it turns out that the famous mathematician Kurt Gödel, whose name we associate with the description 'the discoverer of the incompleteness of arithmetic' (as logicians and mathematicians call it), is not in fact the author of that theorem. Gödel stole the manuscript from his friend Schmidt, who actually did the work and mysteriously disappeared in Vienna. Does this show that, whenever we use the name 'Gödel', we in fact refer to Schmidt? Kripke is adamant that it does not. Thus the definite description does not help us to refer to Gödel.

In conclusion, according to Kripke, names do not refer to objects via definite descriptions; indeed, they do not refer in virtue of their meaning. Rather they refer to objects in a kind of direct way – which is why Kripke's view has sometimes been called (though not by Kripke himself) the direct theory of reference. Strictly speaking, names have no meaning, though we might also say that all there is to their meaning is this reference relation. After all, names presumably contribute to the meaning of the sentences in which they occur. Now you might well ask how this impressive feat of direct reference is accomplished. Kripke's answer to this question is what we examine next. (Note that I use 'reference' to talk about the referential connection between an expression and an object, and 'referent' to talk about the object referred to by an expression.)

4.3   The causal theory of names

Kripke himself preferred to call his view a 'picture' rather than a 'theory', for it was not intended to provide necessary and sufficient conditions for reference. (I'll stick to 'theory' in what follows, bearing this caveat in mind.) The basic idea is that our success in referring to definite objects by using names ultimately rests on a direct relation that some language user or group of language users had to those objects. For instance, the referent of a person's name may be fixed through an initial baptism and then transmitted from one speaker to another through a chain of communication. Each speaker uses the name with the intention to refer to the object those whom she got the name from refer to, and this leads back to the object initially baptized. Our use of 'Aristotle' is based on a long chain of communication that, eventually, is directly connected to Aristotle. The chain is much shorter when, say, one of my relatives uses my name to refer to me. Often the object is named by ostension, that is, just by being pointed at while it is named. Obviously, no such straightforward initial 'baptism' occurs in the case of most cities, most islands and so on. But a description may also be used to fix the referent of a name; such is perhaps the description 'the land I live in', when used by the inhabitants of a given part of the world to fix the referent of the name they want to use to designate that part. Such a description is not supposed to endow the name with a meaning in virtue of which an object is subsequently picked out. Rather, once the referent is fixed, the description can be abandoned and the object is picked out in virtue of the causal chain that connects the users of the name to the initial naming, and hence to the referent of the name.

Before I proceed to assess the causal theory of names, there is an important distinction I should introduce to make clear what exactly the theory is a theory of. Frege's and Searle's versions of descriptivism, on which

Kripke focuses and to which his theory is a reaction, understand descriptivism both as a theory of meaning for names and as a theory of how names refer. The description or descriptions one associates with a name at once provide the sense or meaning of that name and determine its referent: the referent is either the object that uniquely satisfies the description (as in Frege) or the object that has at least some of the characteristics associated with the name (as in Searle). In both cases it can be said, I think, that it is in virtue of the sense or meaning of names that we succeed in referring to objects by using them. Now, Kripke rejects descriptivism both as a theory of meaning and as a theory of reference and offers his causal theory as an alternative to the descriptivist theory of reference. Does it fare any better?

On the face of it, the causal theory does seem to be an improvement on the cluster theory of reference (and a fortiori on the classical theory). It does not have to maintain, of any set of definite descriptions we might associate with a name, that at least some of them necessarily apply to the object referred to by the name. Indeed, it does not have to maintain that any set of definite descriptions has to be associated with a name for us to use it to refer to an object. The definite descriptions we associate with a name may even fail to apply to the object we have in mind, and yet we may succeed in referring to the object by using the name. Kripke, however, has no alternative theory of meaning for names to offer us. But, as I just said, presumably names contribute to the meaning of the sentences in which they occur. 'Hesperus is Hesperus' does not mean the same as 'Hesperus is Phosphorus', even though the two names co-refer. 'Apollo does not exist' is a meaningful sentence, even though 'Apollo' has no referent. I am not suggesting that these problems can be solved solely through a descriptivist theory, but only that Kripke's view of names is at best incomplete. About Frege's puzzle, perhaps Kripke could say that 'Hesperus' and 'Phosphorus' have been used in different chains of communication, which accounts for the different ways they contribute to the meaning of the sentences in which they occur. The causal chain that leads from the naming of Venus as 'Hesperus' is different from the causal chain that leads from the naming of Venus as 'Phosphorus'. But from this it follows that, when the ignorant person is told that Hesperus is Phosphorus, she learns something about language: that the planet Venus was named in two different ways and that the two names are used to refer to the same object. Frege, however, thought that the identity statement teaches us something about the world: that a certain heavenly body seen in the evening is the same as a certain heavenly body seen in the morning. Be that as it may, the causal view, as it stands, certainly cannot apply to empty names, as there are precisely no objects that such names refer to. Kripke's only goal, however, in the text we have considered, was to give us a better picture of how names refer – better, that is, than the descriptivists' picture. And, to repeat, he did start a revolution in doing so.

To my mind, the most valuable part of the causal theory is its ability to start explaining, at last, how the connections between words (in this case, names; but we'll soon consider predicates) and the world are established – and hence its promise to explain how expressions get to mean what they do by externalizing meaning. Also noteworthy is the fact that the causal theory is a social view, insofar as what objects we refer to when we use names often depends essentially on what other members of our community refer to by those names. (Presumably, though, one could name an object for one's solitary use.) But, in the end, the picture is too crude and therefore still problematic, as was brilliantly argued by the British philosopher Gareth Evans, one year after Kripke's book was published.

4.4   A critique of the causal theory of names

According to Evans, the problems for the causal theory (considered, to be clear, as a theory of reference: it is Kripke's view that Evans is addressing) are, in a nutshell, that it ignores the context in which a proper name is being used as well as the intentions of the speaker in using that name, and that it makes no room for changes of referent, that is, changes in what object is referred to or denoted by a name, which Evans also calls the denotation of the name (I shall use 'denotation' and 'referent' interchangeably in what follows). It is useful here, following Evans, to distinguish between two kinds of theory of denotation that neither the descriptivists nor Kripke clearly separate. One is the theory of what object a speaker denotes when using a name on a particular occasion; call this the theory of speaker denotation. The other is the theory of what a name denotes in a community of speakers; call this the theory of name denotation. It is an interesting question how the two theories might be related. It is certainly tempting to think that a given name came to have a given object as its denotation in a linguistic community because some speaker or group of speakers in that community used the name to denote that object. In other words it is tempting to think that the theory of name denotation rests on the theory of speaker denotation. Be that as it may, Evans introduces examples that respectively tell against each kind of causal theory of denotation.

Recall my earlier suggestion that we can use a name and ask questions and make comments about its referent even though we associate that name only with an indefinite description, which may indeed apply to more than one object (I associate only 'a famous physicist' with 'Feynman', but Feynman is not the only famous physicist). Similarly, I may start using a name to refer to an object in a context in which I hear people use the name to talk about that object. Taking Evans's example, imagine that I hear people use the name 'Louis' to talk about a certain person, Louis, and I become interested in his deeds and sayings. There can be no doubt that it is their Louis – say, Louis XIII – that I am talking about, even if in the conversation I am misled into acquiring thoughts that do not fit that king. This tells in favour of the causal theory: I refer to the object referred to by those from whom I got the name. But suppose lots of time passes and I completely forget this conversation. There is now nothing I can say that connects me to that king. Will I still use 'Louis' to refer to the French king? Suppose I say 'Louis was a good basketball player.' Do I believe that Louis XIII was a basketball player? Am I still talking about that king? Indeed, am I talking about anyone? This example strongly suggests, Evans concludes, that there is something wrong with Kripke's causal theory, considered as a theory of speaker denotation: it ignores the context in which a name is used and makes it sound as if denoting an object is sometimes just a 'magic trick' that can be performed no matter what. It sounds more sensible to say that I was talking about Louis XIII in the original context, but not in the later one. Does the causal theory considered as a theory of name denotation have this kind of problem, however?

Take an actual case, famously exploited by Evans. 'Madagascar' was once used to refer to a part of the African continent, but it is now used to refer to an island off the coast of Africa (supposedly as a result of a misunderstanding of Marco Polo's). Thus the original causal chain that led from a part of the African continent was broken and the denotation of 'Madagascar' changed, which strongly suggests, again, that something is wrong with the causal theory, namely that it ignores the intentions of speakers when they use a name to refer to an object. Evans's idea here is that, when speakers in a community use a name, they must somehow have a certain object in mind and, consequently, must intend the referent of the name to be a certain object – say, a certain part of the African continent, or a certain African island. But does this idea not invite a return to descriptivism, in particular to the cluster version of it? It does not, as Evans insists; for the point is not that the relevant intention is to refer to whatever object uniquely satisfies the majority of descriptions speakers associate with the name. As Evans (1973, p. 197) asks, why indeed should some object, which is 'utterly isolated (causally)' from the speakers' community, be the referent of a name simply because it fits the descriptions associated with that name? Here it is the descriptivist theory that sounds magical, if not 'absurd'! I have been suggesting this much all along, when I asked the descriptivists, repeatedly, how the connections between the descriptions associated with names and their referents are established. Pretty obviously, a relation, presumably causal, between the use of names and their referents has to take place; however, in view of the objections articulated by Evans, it cannot be the crude relation envisaged by Kripke. Consequently Evans proposes another version of the causal theory.

4.5   The causal theory of names revised

According to Evans, Kripke is definitely right in urging that there is a causal relation between speakers and the referents of the names they use. But Kripke, Evans contends, has 'mislocated' the causal relation. The relevant causal relation is not that which obtains between the baptized object and the speaker's use of a name to baptize that object. Rather it is that which obtains between an object's 'states and doings' and the speaker's 'body of information' about that object. The idea is that names come to refer to the objects they refer to because the speakers who use those names intend them to refer to the objects whose states and doings they have causally interacted with and that are thus the source of the information speakers possess about them. Thus we may say that the denotation of a name is fixed by the body of information speakers associate with that name. Crucially, however, the fixing is done by the fact that the information has a certain causal origin, not by the fact that some object happens to satisfy it, as the descriptivist would have it. Now, you may well ask, what makes a body of information the relevant one? Which of the many beliefs an object may cause us to have are the relevant ones, such that they are in turn associated with the name that refers to that object, and who are the holders of these relevant beliefs? I do not think that there are clear-cut answers to these questions, insofar as we may not be able to tell, in advance of the introduction of a name, what kind of particular beliefs may be relevant. But, focusing on the theory of name denotation, as Evans does, it seems reasonable to think that, for every name used in a linguistic community, there will be a speaker or a group of speakers who somehow dictate what those beliefs are and, so, to what objects the names they are associated with refer. These speakers will do so in large part because they are closely connected to the object whose states and doings are responsible for the body of information they associate with the name they use to talk about that object.

(I see no reason to think that this is incompatible with also maintaining that a speaker could use a name to talk about an object and everyone manages to understand what object the speaker is talking about, even though no one else uses that name to talk about that object. This is to say that the use of a name does not have to be social in order to succeed in referring to an object, even though, as a matter of highly practical fact, many uses of names are social – by and large we share the bodies of information associated with names and, if this information is lacking, we rely on others, from whom we got the names.)

Here is an example from Evans that illustrates the intricacies of his version of the causal theory. Suppose that a young man A, nicknamed 'Turnip', leaves the village in which he was born and raised. Suppose that fifty years later another man B turns up and settles as a hermit at the edge of the village. Three or four of the villagers who are still alive and who knew Turnip falsely believe that Turnip has returned and start using 'Turnip' among themselves as well as with younger members of their community, who know nothing about the origin of the name. Now suppose that the older villagers figure out that the hermit is not A. Presumably, according to Evans, they will say 'It isn't Turnip after all' rather than 'It appears that Turnip did not come from this village.' All along, they have been talking about A, albeit saying many false things about him, such as 'Here is Turnip coming over for his morning coffee.' A is what Evans calls the 'dominant' source of the information they associate with 'Turnip'. However, when the older villagers die, B may well become the dominant source of the information the younger villagers associate with 'Turnip', and thus the referent of the name as they use it.

In the end, Evans's theory may leave us dissatisfied insofar as it remains nebulous just how the relevant connections between speakers' use of names and their referents are selected. Yet, to my mind, Evans's version of the causal theory is a vast improvement over Kripke's, not to mention the descriptivist theory. Interestingly, as I see it, Evans is trying to have the best of each approach: the causal theorist's and the descriptivist's. On the one hand, the body of information or beliefs associated with a name are caused by the object referred to by the name. Thus something of the causal theory is being saved. On the other hand, we may think of the body of information or beliefs associated with a name as playing a role similar to the role the descriptivists wanted from descriptions. Thus, something of the descriptivist theory is being saved. To be clear, however, contra the descriptivists we have focused on, the body of information or descriptions are not necessarily true of the object we refer to with a name. They just happen to be true of the object and, as a result, help us to refer to the object. Moreover, as I see it, they help to understand how a name can have meaning, at least insofar as it contributes to the meaning of the sentences in which it occurs: this is due in part to the body of information we associate with it and to our use of sentences to express this body of information.

It should be stressed that the difference between the descriptivist theory and Evans's causal theory is extremely critical and accounts for the progress we have made in our search for an answer to the question what makes it possible for linguistic expressions to have meaning. For we now know something about the beliefs in virtue of which we use names to refer to objects and, as I just suggested, in virtue of which we use them meaningfully: they come from states and doings of the objects themselves, with which we have interacted causally. Meaning has been externalized and thereby to some extent illuminated. This has taken about eight decades to come about (if we leave aside some early signs of externalism that can be found in Wittgenstein). But eight decades is a short time in the history of philosophy!

The progress we have accomplished so far is limited, however. What we need to investigate next is that in virtue of which bodies of information, beliefs, and descriptions get to mean what they do. What we need to investigate next is the meaning of predicates or general terms – that is, terms that may apply to more than one object. As we are about to see, an externalist account can be provided here too.

4.6 The causal theory of general terms

The kind of externalist view Kripke was proposing was not meant to apply just to proper names but to general terms as well. Such a view was developed, at about the same time, not only by Kripke but also by another American philosopher, Hilary Putnam, whom I shall focus on here.

What initially motivated Putnam's inquiry is two assumptions on which he took the traditional picture of meaning to rest and that, he argued, cannot be met jointly by any notion of meaning: (1) 'knowing the meaning of a term is just a matter of being in a certain psychological state'; and (2) 'the meaning of a term determines its extension' (Putnam, 1973, p. 700). 'Extension' is often used to talk about the set of things a general term applies to. Thus the meaning of a term determines the set of things it applies to; for example, it is in virtue of its meaning *tiger* that 'tiger' applies to all tigers – past, present and future. To be sure, Frege, who is one of the traditional philosophers Putnam was targeting, did maintain that meaning (or sense) determines extension: what our words apply to depends on their senses, on what we mean by these words, so that if two words have the same meaning they have the same extension. But Putnam thought that, even though Frege located senses in a third, abstract realm, he was committed to the first assumption as well; for our minds have to grasp the senses that our words are connected with, if we are to use words meaningfully. Putnam recommended that we abandon the first assumption: meanings are not – at least, as we'll see, not entirely – in the head, as he provocatively put it; and he argued that the essential ingredient of meaning is extension, so that the second assumption can be kept: if the meaning of a term essentially depends on the set of items to which it applies, it seems to follow, trivially, that the meaning of a term determines its extension. Thus, since the extension of general terms is comprised of items in the world around us, meaning is, again, going to be externalized. How does Putnam proceed to do this?

Putnam focuses his argument on natural kind words such as 'water', 'gold', 'lemon' – words that are about things to be found in nature and that typically have a fundamental, underlying structure, an 'essence' that can be revealed by science – rather than on words for artefacts such as 'pencil', 'chair', 'bottle', though he thinks that his argument applies to these words as well. Putnam's argument is supposed to be a rather intuitive one, based as it was on a thought experiment that has become famous: the Twin Earth thought experiment.

Putnam invites us to imagine that somewhere in the galaxy there is a planet – call it Twin Earth – that is like our planet Earth in all respects, except that the liquid called 'water' on Twin Earth is not composed of H_2O but of XYZ molecules. XYZ has all the superficial macroscopic properties that H_2O has: it tastes, looks and feels like water, quenches thirst like water, supports sailing and swimming like water and so on. But the oceans and lakes and rivers of Twin Earth are filled with XYZ and not with water, it rains XYZ on Twin Earth and not water, people bathe in XYZ on Twin Earth and not in water, and so on – or so Putnam describes the situation (note the assumption, implicit in the description of the thought experiment, that only H_2O can be water, which may seem to some to be question-begging). Consequently, according to Putnam, 'water' as used by an Earthian has a different meaning from that of 'water' as used by a Twin Earthian. Imagine, indeed, that we were to visit Twin Earth. We may at first assume that 'water' as used by Twin Earthians means the same as our 'water', but upon discovering that their 'water' refers to XYZ we would change our mind, or so Putnam contends. We would think that a difference in the chemical composition of the liquid referred to by the word 'water' would make for a difference in the meaning of this word. In addition to this, considering that the extension of 'water' on either planet did not change from 1750 to 1950, we would conclude that, even in 1750, when no one could have yet discovered that the chemical formulae of the two liquids are different, 'water' on Twin Earth meant something different from 'water' on Earth. Finally, it is noteworthy that, according to Putnam, the Earthian and the Twin Earthian mean different things even though they are in the same brain states – since they are supposed to be, molecule for molecule, identical (forgetting about the water component!). It follows that to mean something by a word cannot simply depend on being in a certain brain state. More importantly for Putnam's argument, the Earthian and the Twin Earthian mean different things by 'water', even though in 1750 they may have been – and in fact were – in the same psychological states when they thought and talked about water. This shows that knowing the meaning of a word is not just a matter of being in a certain psychological state; assumption (1) must be rejected. Moreover, assumption (2) can be kept: as already suggested, since the set of items a word applies to is the essential ingredient of its meaning, it is easy to see how the meaning of a word can in turn determine its extension. What is not clear, however, is just what the argument for this externalist thesis is, apart from the intuitive assumption it relies on.

The crucial question is, who is to say what the extension of a word is? How does it get to be established? Why, as Putnam himself asks, should we accept that 'water' has the same extension in 1750 and in 1950, namely H_2O on Earth and XYZ on Twin Earth? Why could its extension not change between 1750 and 1950? Why, we might further ask, should we accept that 'water' has a different extension on Earth and Twin Earth even in 1950? Putnam's answer is that 'water' refers to the liquid present in the environment of those who have used the word regularly to refer to the liquid. If he were to explain the meaning of 'water' to someone by means of an ostensive definition, he would assume that the liquid he is pointing to is the same kind of liquid as the liquid that he and other speakers in his linguistic community have called 'water' on other occasions. The next question is, then, what does it take for a liquid to be the same kind of liquid as another? Putnam's answer is that this is something for scientists to figure out. What he has no doubt about, though, is that what kind of liquid a liquid is is determined by that liquid's actual, real nature; and, if the real nature – that is, the microstructure – of what is called 'water' on Earth is in fact H_2O, there is no possible world in which water is not H_2O.

There is thus what Putnam calls a 'rigid' element and an 'indexical' element to the meaning of natural kind words. Like proper names, they are rigid designators – they refer to the same stuff – liquid, fruit, metal, animal, tree and so on – in every possible world in which that stuff exists. And what determines what that stuff is to begin with is the actual environment in which the word has been used to talk about the stuff in question. So something is water if it is the same liquid as the liquid we call water on Earth. 'Water' means what it does because it refers to that liquid. Again, meaning has been externalized. The meaning of our words essentially depends on the items in the world around us that we talk about when we use those words – items with which we interact causally in a variety of ways. Crucially, however, how Putnam conceives of what falls into the extension of a natural kind word is rather narrow: the sets of items natural kind words apply to depend only on the real fundamental nature of those items (he admits, though, that some natural kinds may not have a hidden structure). Superficial properties of those items, for example the wetness of water, may help us in acquiring the words for them, but these properties are not essential to what we mean by the words. This view seems immediately to pose a problem: many of us do not know the real nature of the items we talk about, which suggests that many of us do not know what we mean by our words (as Putnam is in fact willing to concede). At the very least, many of us have an incomplete understanding of our own words. What are we to make of this?

4.7   Assessing the causal theory of general terms

Importantly, Putnam seems to include an intentional aspect in his description of how the meanings of natural kind words get fixed. (This is not always recognized even by Putnam himself, which makes his view look more magical than it is.) People, when they use 'water', intend to refer to a certain liquid in their environment. But what identifies a liquid is its microstructure. Do people also intend to refer to the liquid in their environment as having a certain microstructure? Perhaps the scientifically minded do, but what about the others? How are we to decide? What these questions suggest is that the account of meaning Putnam is offering works well as an account of how the scientific meaning of words is determined, perhaps of how language captures or represents the world 'as it really is', as some philosophers might say. But the primary function of language is not to provide an accurate description of the world; it is to communicate. And people have all kinds of reasons for wanting to communicate besides describing the world as it really is, central among them being one that has to do with the ways in which the world affects us. Or perhaps I should say that the world can be described as real in multifarious ways, which different people have an interest in communicating about.

Recall my earlier suggestion that the contribution of a name to the meaning of the sentences in which it occurs is explained by the body of information caused by the item to which the name refers, its 'states and doings'.

Presumably it is not a single belief that we associate with a name but several, and some of them are more significant than others. Why not say the same thing about general terms – namely that we associate with them beliefs about characteristics of the items they refer to? The question I asked earlier was: how do we select the relevant beliefs, and whose beliefs are they? In the case of natural kind words, why should they be beliefs about the real, fundamental nature of the items around us, and why should they thus be the beliefs of the scientifically discerning members of a linguistic community? Communication might be better served if we pay attention to the beliefs of the speaker who uses the word. There is, then, a whole range of possibilities. Sticking to 'water', at one extremity there is the scientist, who knows that water is H_2O and can thus associate this piece of information with 'water'. Then there is the scientist of 1750, who knows that natural kinds have a hidden structure, though she does not yet know that of the liquid she calls 'water'. This belief, too, may contribute to what she means by 'water'. At the other extremity there is the person who has no scientific inclination whatsoever and just wants a glass of the clear liquid that flows out of the spring. Why should a belief she fails to have, and thus an intention she fails to have – namely the intention to refer to the liquid around as having a certain microstructure – play a role in determining what she means by 'water'? It might be replied that, although she does not have that intention, she does intend to refer to what the experts in her community refer to by 'water'. Perhaps she does, perhaps she does not. But, even if she does, it is not clear how much weight that intention should be given. This is best illustrated by another famous thought experiment, developed by the American philosopher Tyler Burge at the end of the 1970s.

This thought experiment is worth presenting in part because it introduces another attempt to externalize meaning: a social way, rather than a physical way. Burge invited us to imagine two linguistic communities identical in all respects, except for the fact that in the actual community – ours – 'arthritis' conventionally means *inflammation of the joints* only, whereas in the counterfactual community 'arthritis' conventionally means *inflammation of the joints or muscles*. Now, suppose that we have two identical individuals, one in each community, uttering the words 'I've got arthritis in my thigh' (Burge, 1979, pp. 77–9). Is each individual expressing the same belief? Burge has no doubt that they are not. The actual individual has a false belief, as one cannot have arthritis in the thigh, whereas the counterfactual individual may well have a true belief, if it turns out that she has an inflammation of the thigh. This is because 'arthritis' means something different in each community. And what an individual who belongs in one or the other community means by a word depends on the conventional meaning of the word in that community.

One reason Burge gives in favour of his conclusion is the one broached earlier: people defer to other members of their community, in this case to medical experts, when they use their words. They use them with the intention to mean what those who know better mean by them. To reiterate my initial reaction, I think that this may be the case, but then it may not. However, even if it is, why should we give more weight to this intention to defer that, we assume, our actual individual has than to her intention to mean by 'arthritis' an ailment that affects both thighs and muscles? Granted, ignoring the former intention may be unscientific: for one thing, the causes of the respective ailments may be different (though this does not seem to bother the experts of the counterfactual community!). But interpreting her as meaning something different from what the experts mean could make for smoother communication and would not require us to say that she has an incomplete understanding of her

word, as we often might be required to say if we interpret
speakers Burge's way. Here is a personal anecdote to
illustrate the point. A rheumatologist once told me that
he had a patient whose understanding of 'arthritis' was
similar to our actual individual's. The rheumatologist did
not try to correct his patient's use, but interpreted her as
meaning *inflammation of joints or muscles* by 'arthritis',
as she herself did, and proceeded to use the word in the
same way in conversations with her. This goes to show
that people do not always speak conventionally and
are perfectly understood all the same. And this strongly
suggests that what is essential to meaning is that in
virtue of which people communicate with each other.
(That communication does not require that they mean
the same thing by the same word was already suggested
with the example of 'epitaph' in Chapter 2. I shall return
to that claim in Chapter 7.)

Where does all this leave us?

To begin with, let me emphasize the difference
between the social externalism of Burge and the physical
externalism of Putnam. With Burge, the meaning of a
general term is fixed conventionally – contra Putnam,
for whom it is fixed only by the world itself. As a result,
Burge's experts have a complete understanding of what
they mean, whereas Putnam's experts may not – they
certainly did not have a complete understanding of
'water' in 1750. But Burge and Putnam have something
important in common: they are both committed to
saying that intentions or beliefs that belong to people
other than the speakers and that speakers lack may play
an essential role in determining what speakers mean by
their words; as Putnam (1975, p. 227) famously said,
meanings 'just ain't in the head'. And both give the
intention to speak like those who know best a primary
role to play. I have expressed reservations about each
claim. To take the second one first, I do not see how
to justify the claim that the intention to mean the same
as others should override the intention to use words

with a certain meaning. And I do not see how to justify the claim that beliefs or intentions that a speaker does not have should play a role in determining what she means by her words. Indeed, I would rather understand extension in such a way as to render Putnam's two initial assumptions compatible. On the one hand, meanings can be completely in the head: knowing the meaning of a term is just a matter of being in a psychological state. On the other hand, however, this psychological state has been caused by an aspect of the term's extension that is not necessarily its real nature, and so meaning can still determine extension. Thus, to be clear, I am suggesting that we not take the only meaning-determinant aspect of the items that fall into a given extension to be the real nature of the items. My scientifically oblivious person could be talking both about H_2O and XYZ when she uses 'water', depending on what aspects of the liquid referred to by 'water' she takes to be relevant – after all, H_2O and XYZ have all their phenomenal properties in common.

Perhaps we should distinguish between the theory of what words mean conventionally or scientifically and the theory of what speakers mean by their words, just as we distinguished between the theory of name denotation and the theory of speaker denotation. Deep down, however, we want to know how speakers come to mean what they do by their words, since it is speakers, after all, who ultimately establish the conventional or expert meanings of their linguistic community. Even if we accepted Burge's account, we would not have a complete account of meaning, for we need to know how linguistic conventions come about. More importantly, even if we accepted all of Putnam's account, we still would not have a complete account of meaning (though the physical side of externalism seems to bring us closer to a complete account). For what Putnam does is explain the meaning of certain words by taking the meaning of some others for granted. How do we come to mean what we do by 'liquid', 'wet', 'ocean', and so on? If I want to define 'water' ostensively, I cannot simply point at a bunch of water, say, the Atlantic Ocean, and say 'This is called "water".' I must at the very least say 'This liquid is called "water"', or it must be understood that it is the name of a liquid that is being defined. Without the background of a language, this definition might as well be taken to be the definition of 'wet', of 'ocean', and so on. Thus it is not, presumably, through direct connections between our use of words and various objects or aspects of objects in the world that the meaning of words gets established. How, then, does it work? In the next chapter I investigate a possible answer to this question that may be an improvement on Putnam's externalist view.

References

Burge, Tyler. 1979. 'Individualism and the Mental'. *Midwest Studies in Philosophy*, 4(1): 73–121.

Evans, Gareth. 1973. 'The Causal Theory of Names'. *Aristotelian Society Supplementary Volumes*, 47(1): 187–208.

Kripke, Saul. 1980. *Naming and Necessity*. Blackwell.

Putnam, Hilary. 1973. 'Meaning and Reference'. *Journal of Philosophy*, 70(19): 699–711.

Putnam, Hilary. 1975. 'The Meaning of "Meaning"', in his *Mind, Language and Reality: Philosophical Papers*, vol. 2. Cambridge University Press, 215–271.

Searle, John. 1958. 'Proper Names'. *Mind*, 67(266): 166–173.

Further Readings

Searle's further discussion of proper names and his response to Kripke:

Searle, John. 1982. 'Proper Names and Intentionality'. *Pacific Philosophical Quarterly*, 63(3): 205–225.

Kripke's further discussion of his view on proper names:
Kripke, Saul. 2018. *Reference and Existence: The John Locke Lectures*. Oxford University Press.

Evans's further discussion of his view on proper names:
Evans, Gareth. 1982. *The Varieties of Reference*. Oxford University Press.

Revisiting the two externalist thought experiments:
Burge, Tyler. 2007 [1982]. 'Two Thought Experiments Reviewed', in his *Foundations of Mind: Philosophical Essays*, vol. 2. Oxford University Press, 182–191.

Critiques of the kind of externalism discussed in the chapter:
Davidson, Donald. 2001 [1987]. 'Knowing One's Own Mind', in his *Subjective, Intersubjective, Objective*. Oxford University Press, 15–38.
Wikforss, Åsa. 2004. 'Externalism and Incomplete Understanding'. *Philosophical Quarterly*, 54(215): 287–294.

A comprehensive introduction to externalism:
Kallestrup, Jesper. 2012. *Semantic Externalism*. Routledge.

5

Meaning and Truth

As I said in the introductory chapter, we might think of the questions addressed by philosophers of language as falling into two broad categories: one has to do with the relation between meaning and extralinguistic reality, the other has to do with the relation between meaning and language users. So far, we have focused on attempts to answer questions that belong to the first category. And, through the examination of externalist views, we have made progress towards answering our initial and fundamental question – the question of what it is for words to mean what they do. We still lack, however, a full understanding of how the connections between language and the world around us, connections essential to meaning according to externalism, are established and maintained. As I asked at the end of the previous chapter, if all we are allowed to do in order to endow a word with meaning is point at some item in our environment, how do we get to mean, say, *water* by 'water' – rather than *ocean*, or *wet*, or *liquid*? And, if we are allowed to say that the word we are defining is one that names a liquid, whence the meaning of 'liquid'?

A distinctive element of Kripke's and Putnam's externalist views is that their focus is on connections between particular entities or properties in the world around us and the words we use to refer to them. Evans's externalist view is notably different, as its focus is on connections between the states and doings of particular entities and the words we use to refer to the entities whose states and doings they are. Evans discusses only ordinary proper names, but I suggested that the kind of connection he deems relevant between them and the entities they refer to could be extended to general terms: the relevant connections could be between our use of these terms and some of the characteristics of the items that the terms refer to. To put it more precisely, the relevant connections could be those that obtain between the bodies of information we associate with the words we use to refer to those items and features of the items themselves, namely features that cause those bodies of information. This, in turn, suggests that the relevant meaning-determining connections are those that obtain between the use of sentences and the states of affairs and events they purport to be about, since bodies of information are composed of beliefs expressed by sentences. Hence the suggestion is that the crucial connection to investigate in order to get clearer about the nature of meaning is the one between meaning and truth, since the idea is that what determines meaning in the first instance is what in the world is the case – say, that water is wet – or what in the world is happening – say, that Jim is drinking water – in short, what it is in the world that makes our sentences true.

As I also said in the introductory chapter, a good topic to pursue is what the relation is between the two broad categories of questions addressed by philosophers of language. And I suggested that the first category – questions to do with the relation between meaning and extralinguistic reality – might be more fruitfully addressed by considering the second category – questions to do with the relation between meaning and language users. So far, leaving aside chapter 2 (whose goal was to isolate the notion of meaning we are focusing on), and granting that all the philosophers studied in chapter 4 recognize the role played by the intentions of speakers when they use words meaningfully, little has been said about language users, not to mention that we have no clue as to what determines the meaning of the intentions themselves. In particular, little has been said about how people communicate through language. But communication, as I started suggesting in chapter 4, may be the most significant aspect of language to scrutinize in a study of linguistic meaning. After all, meanings are what we attach to the sounds or marks we produce in order to communicate. This suggests that a study of how we communicate linguistically may shed light on the question what makes meaning possible. The suggestion that we pay close attention to communication also reinforces the idea that it is sentences rather than sub-sentential expressions such as names or general terms that we should be focusing on. For, normally, it is sentences that we utter in order to communicate linguistically and convey information about the world around us and our states of mind – in short, in order to get things done.

In this chapter we start examining the views of a philosopher we encountered in chapter 2: Donald Davidson, who emphasized both the connection between meaning and truth and the primary role communication has to play in our philosophical understanding of meaning.

5.1   From truth to meaning

Starting in the late 1960s, Davidson brought about another revolution in the history of philosophy of language. Most striking was the novelty of his approach to perennial questions about meaning. Unlike Kripke and Putnam, who relied heavily on intuitions about hypothetical cases for their account of meaning, Davidson based his approach on the assumption that everything that belongs to meaning is essentially public and that language is essentially communicable. Hence inquiring into how we communicate with one another is bound to shed light on the nature of meaning. Furthermore, Davidson was also keen on providing an account of meaning that is not question-begging, that is, an account that would not employ from the start the very notion the inquiry is trying to illuminate. So, he thinks, it is a good idea to begin by reflecting not just on how people communicate with one another but on how we could interpret an alien speaker from scratch, without the help of a bilingual interpreter or dictionary. The assumption here is that reflecting on what it takes to understand a speaker whose language we initially do not know will shed light on what it takes for words to mean what they do. This in turn rests, of course, on the assumption that language is essentially communicable, but this assumption is not exactly outrageous. The idea is not that we always succeed in communicating, or that we always do so smoothly, but that by and large we do communicate with one another and that, in principle at least, it is always possible for us to do so. Everyday life depends on that.

In light of these assumptions, Davidson submits that we could answer the question what it is for words to mean what they do in a philosophically interesting way if we knew how to construct a theory that satisfies two demands: (1) it would enable us to interpret, that is, understand, all the utterances, actual and potential, of a speaker or group of speakers; and (2) it would be built without prior knowledge not only of the language of the speaker but also of the detailed 'propositional attitudes' of the speaker, that is, her beliefs, desires, intentions, fears, hopes and the like. All these are attitudes that can be expressed by sentences that appear in that-clauses, as the sentence 'it is raining now in Toronto' appears in 'Jim believes that it is raining now in Toronto', and all are attitudes towards the contents of these that-clauses. These contents are sometimes called 'propositions' by philosophers, whence the expression 'propositional attitude'. For Davidson, basing our interpretation on detailed knowledge of the propositional attitudes of the speaker would be question-begging, given the close relation between the content of those attitudes and the meaning of the sentences used to express them.

The theory whose construction we are to reflect on in order ultimately to answer the question what it is for words to mean what they do is an empirical theory, based on evidence concerning the speaker for whom it is a theory. It does not itself tell us anything about the nature of meaning, about what makes it possible for words to have meaning. If we were to write it down, it would simply give us – describe, as it were – the meanings of all the basic linguistic expressions of a speaker; and it would do so in such a way that we could understand all the utterances of a speaker. It is reflecting on the *construction* of such a theory that will yield a philosophical understanding of the nature of meaning. Thus 'theory of meaning', as it is used in this context, is ambiguous: it is either the theory of interpretation that we are building to interpret a speaker or the theory of the nature of meaning that, Davidson thinks, is afforded by the building of the theory of interpretation. The former is often referred to as a 'semantic' theory, the latter as a 'foundational' or 'meta-semantic' theory. I shall usually stick to 'theory of interpretation' to designate the theory that is to be constructed; and I shall use 'account of meaning' to designate the foundational theory, which is the primary object of our inquiry.

How are we to fulfil the first condition on an acceptable theory of interpretation? Why, to begin with, must it be met? Pretty obviously, this is because, once they have mastered a finite vocabulary and a finite set of rules, language users are prepared to produce and to understand a potentially infinite number of sentences. So an adequate theory of interpretation must enable us to produce and to understand such an infinity. (Recall that our ability to do this is one of the distinctive linguistic facts that an adequate account of the nature of meaning has at least to make room for, as I said in chapter 2.) The theory of interpretation could be used to achieve this feat if it is a compositional theory, that is, a theory that shows how the meaning of any particular sentence or complex expression depends on the meaning of its simple parts – or 'semantical primitives', as Davidson calls the expressions whose meaning does not have to be explained by reference to other expressions – and on the way they are combined. For instance, the meaning of 'Socrates is wise' is explained by appealing to the meanings of the name 'Socrates' and the predicate 'is wise'. Thus a language that can be used to produce and understand a potentially infinite number of sentences must have a finite number of semantical primitives and rules of composition, each of which could appear in different combinations in different sentences; for example 'Socrates' could appear in 'Socrates is a philosopher' and 'is wise' could appear in 'Aristotle is wise.' A theory of interpretation for such a language must have a finite number of axioms, each one providing the meaning of a primitive or a rule. The meaning-giving theorems are generated from these axioms. (I'll soon illustrate this with the help of a simplified language.)

Turning to the theorems that such a theory generates, what are they supposed to look like? Even though they are supposed to give the meaning of each sentence of the language under study and to be derived from axioms that are supposed to give the meaning of each simple part of that language, they cannot themselves involve the notion of meaning; in particular, they cannot be sentences of the form 's means that p' (where 's' is replaced by the name of a sentence and 'p' is replaced by a sentence that gives the meaning of s). The main problem with a theorem of this kind is that 'means that' introduces a context in which the substitution of one true that-clause for another need not preserve the truth value of the whole sentence. Thus we cannot substitute 'Grass is green' for 'Snow is white' after 'means that' in '"Snow is white" means that snow is white', even though 'Snow is white' and 'Grass is green' are both true. And the reason why we cannot substitute is that 'Snow is white' and 'Grass is green' do not have the same meaning. (This is similar to what we saw in chapter 3: we cannot substitute 'Ortcutt is a spy' for 'the man in the brown hat is a spy' in 'Ralph believes that the man in the brown hat is a spy', even though both that-clauses are true of the same person; for 'Ortcutt' and 'the man in the brown hat' do not have the same meaning.) Now, the problem here is that we are appealing to the notion of meaning in order to explain why we cannot substitute expressions in certain contexts. But, if building a theory of interpretation is to yield an account of meaning, we should not have to appeal to the notion of meaning in order to explain any of its distinctive characteristics. Davidson proposes that a theory that does not raise that problem but that nevertheless does everything we want from a theory of interpretation should take the form of a specific kind of theory of truth: that put forward by the Polish logician Alfred Tarski.

The Tarskian theory of truth is not a theory of the nature of truth or an analysis of the concept of truth. It is a theory supposed to generate, for each sentence of the language for which it holds, the conditions under which that sentence is true. Thus it is supposed to generate sentences of the form 's is true if and only if p'. These are known as 'T-sentences', where 's' is the name of a sentence of the language under study (the 'object language') and 'p' is a sentence of the language used to give the theory of interpretation of the object language (the 'metalanguage'). In what follows I shall use the expression 'iff', which stands for 'if and only if'. For instance:

T   'Snow is white' is true iff snow is white.

Note that the sentence of the object language (the sentence on the left-hand side) is being mentioned – we are saying something about the sentence, namely that it is true – and the sentence of the metalanguage (the sentence on the right-hand side) is being used – we are saying something about the world, namely that snow is white. Davidson's goal is to show that a theory that generates truth conditions, if properly constructed, can be used as a theory of interpretation because the sentence of the metalanguage can give the meaning of the sentence of the object language. You may think that this is trivially true: 'Snow is white' obviously means *snow is white*. Right, but that is only because 'Snow is white' is a sentence of English. It is important to keep in mind that the object language will typically be different from the metalanguage.

The generation of the T-sentences is based on a finite number of axioms, which give the semantic properties of all the simple expressions and their modes of combination, that is, which tell us how they contribute to the truth conditions – and hence the meaning – of the sentences in which they occur. Thus the axioms for all the predicates and singular terms of the language under study tell us what those words apply to or designate. And the axioms for truth-functional connectives such as 'and' and for quantifiers such as 'all' show how these terms contribute to the truth conditions of the sentences in which they occur. The basic idea is to match each semantical primitive of the language of the speaker (the object language) with an expression of the language used to construct the theory of interpretation for that language (the metalanguage). To illustrate, imagine a very simplified version of French, with only five axioms (and no grammatical gender):

> 'Bardot' (in French) designates Bardot.
>
> 'Est une actrice' (in French) applies to an object iff the object is an actress.
>
> 'Est française' (in French) applies to an object iff the object is French.
>
> 'Est bonne' (in French) applies to an object iff the object is good.
>
> For any sentences S1 and S2, the sentence resulting from using 'et' to join S1 and S2 is true (in French) iff S1 is true and S2 is true.

From these axioms we must be able to derive the theorems or T-sentences of the theory. For instance:

> T   'Bardot est une actrice' is true (in French) iff Bardot is an actress.

We can derive this T-sentence because we have checked the axioms for 'Bardot' and for 'est une actrice' and accordingly determined that we can replace 'Bardot' with 'Bardot' and 'est une actrice' with 'is an actress' to express the truth conditions of 'Bardot est une actrice.' It looks as if we can also give the truth conditions of 'Bardot est une actrice française', since we can analyse it as 'Bardot est française et Bardot est une actrice', for which the truth conditions are:

> T   'Bardot est française et Bardot est une actrice' is true (in French) iff 'Bardot is French' is true and 'Bardot is an actress' is true.

But 'Bardot est une bonne actrice' cannot be analysed as 'Bardot est bonne et Bardot est une actrice.' (To make it more obvious: 'Bardot is a good actress' cannot be analysed as 'Bardot is good' and 'Bardot is an actress.') This is one of the many difficulties Davidson's approach has to confront: how to give the truth conditions of sentences that contain attributive adjectives such as 'good'? With our simple language, the difficulty might be surmountable just by adding an axiom to our list: 'good actress'. But it is unlikely that this will do for our ordinary, much more complex languages. Think of the unlimited number of predicates that 'good' could modify: 'good conversationalist', 'good friend', 'good musician' . . . How could we ever have a finite list of axioms?

The problem of how to fit attributive adjectives into the theory of truth is not the only one Davidson had to cope with. For one thing, the theory seems to apply only to declarative sentences, as only they can be true or false and thus have truth conditions. How, then, do we deal with imperative sentences such as 'Bring me the book on the table', or with interrogative sentences such as 'Is there any salt'? How do we deal with sentences of reported speech, whose truth value does not depend on the truth value of the that-clause? For instance, the truth value of 'Jim believes that it is raining now in Toronto' does not depend on the truth value of 'It is raining now in Toronto.' It may be true that Jim believes that even though it is not raining now in Toronto. There was a very active research program, in the 1970s and 1980s, that tried to address these and many other problems. Davidson himself tried to solve many of them, often successfully. For instance, he analysed sentences that contain a demonstrative element such as 'this' by relating the truth conditions of the sentences in which the demonstrative occurs to changing speakers and times. Thus:

T   'This book was stolen' is true as (potentially) spoken by speaker s at time t iff the book demonstrated [i.e. indicated or indexed] by s at t is stolen prior to t.

But he could not solve them all. He came in fact to acknowledge that they could not all be solved; yet he thought that a Tarski-style theory of truth could be made to work as a theory of interpretation for central parts of language, and so he did not abandon the idea that reflecting on how to build it would afford central insights into the nature of meaning. The construction of the theory is what we examine next. This is where 'radical interpretation', the interpretation of an alien speaker from scratch, is introduced.

5.2   Radical interpretation

What we have established so far is the form a theory of interpretation should take, according to Davidson. It should be a Tarski-style theory of truth, which has a finite number of axioms; and from these the truth conditions can be derived of many, if not all, of the sentences of the language for which it is a theory (these are known as the 'formal constraints' on the theory). The next question is how this theory should be built, such that it may be used as a theory of interpretation, which is to say, such that the theorems or T-sentences derived from the axioms of the theory are meaning-giving. After all, a biconditional, a sentence of the form 's iff p', understood in the logical 'material' mode, as Davidson understands it, is true if each side of the biconditional is true (or each side is false). Thus '"Snow is white" is true iff grass is green' is a true sentence. (It is true that the sentence 'Snow is white' is true, and it is true that grass is green.) But obviously 'Snow is white' does not mean *grass is green*, and so this T-sentence cannot be meaning giving. Thus we'll have to make sure that the axioms of the theory we have built do not entail this kind of T-sentence. To see how such a proper theory could be built, Davidson, inspired by W. V. O. Quine, embarks on the thought experiment of radical interpretation.

The thought experiment is supposed to show how we could interpret an alien speaker from scratch, that is, recall, without prior knowledge of her language or without detailed knowledge of her beliefs and other propositional attitudes. The theory, also recall, is supposed to be empirical. We are to imagine that we

are building a Tarski-style theory of truth for a speaker
on the basis of the evidence plausibly available to
us. But what evidence could be available to a radical
interpreter? The trouble is that we have to figure out
what the speaker means and what she believes all at
once. If we knew what she believes, we might be able to
figure out what she means by her utterances, and if we
knew what she means by her utterances, we might be
able to figure out what she believes. Thus, if we knew
that she believes that the cat is on the mat, we might be
able to figure out that she means *the cat is on the mat*
by her utterance 'The cat is on the mat.' And if we knew
what she means when she utters 'The cat is on the mat',
we might be able to figure out that she believes that the
cat is on the mat. But we know neither what she believes
nor what she means. What evidence, then, can we use to
break into the circle of meanings and beliefs?

Davidson proposes that we use as evidence the
speaker's attitude of 'holding true' the sentence she
utters at a given time and in given circumstances. To use
a famous example from Quine (admittedly simplifying,
as 'when and only when' is surely too strong):

E   S holds true 'Gavagai' at t when and only when S is
    causally affected by a rabbit at t.

Holding a sentence true is believing it, but detecting
the holding-true attitude is not tantamount to detecting
the content of the attitude. The idea is that the interpreter
can somehow discover that a speaker is expressing a
belief but not know which belief it is. Now, the crucial
question is how we are to go from E to T:

T   'Gavagai' is true as spoken by s at t iff there is a rabbit
    in the vicinity of s at t.

And the short answer is: not in a straightforward way!

According to Davidson, we have to employ something
that philosophers call the 'principle of charity' (mis-
leadingly named this way, since we have no choice but

to employ it). This means that we have to assume, to begin with, that the beliefs the speaker expresses by the sentences she holds true are, typically, the beliefs we also have in the circumstances in which she utters those sentences. We connect her utterances with features of the environment we share with her – for example, with an external event that causes us to form a certain belief and that, we assume, causes her to have that belief, too. Thus, if there is a rabbit passing by and the speaker utters 'Gavagai!', we may initially assume that she is expressing the belief that a rabbit is passing by, for this is what we believe in the circumstances. Pretty obviously, however, before we come up even tentatively with something like T, we'll have to have observed our speaker use the expression 'Gavagai' (or parts of it, if it has parts) on several occasions, in different circumstances, and together with other expressions, which themselves will have been used on several occasions, in different circumstances, and together with other expressions. The first time the speaker utters 'Gavagai', there would be little reason for us to think that she means to be talking about a rabbit. It could be that she means to be talking more generally about its status as an animal, or more specifically about its speed, or its fur, or its ears, or its legs, or the carrot it is holding in its mouth. She could even mean to be talking about a cat, because she has on this one occasion mistaken a rabbit for a cat.

This indicates that the principle of charity is much more complex than my initial description suggests. Most importantly, the principle of charity is holistic: it applies to the detection, not of single beliefs, but of sets of beliefs. We have to determine not only whether the belief the speaker may express by her utterance is justified in the circumstances – say, whether she knows that her position in the environment does not prevent her from distinguishing between rabbits and cats – but also whether this belief is consistent with other beliefs she has – say, whether she also believes that the object that is causing her to utter 'Gavagai' is an animal. If not, we may be mistaken in attributing to her the belief that it is a rabbit; she could mean to be talking about an artefact. Next, for us to attribute to her beliefs about animals and, so, eventually to interpret some expression of hers as meaning *animal*, we'll have to attribute to her beliefs about, say, creatures that are alive; and so on and so forth. In short, when we are radically interpreting, we should look, not just for true beliefs the speaker may be expressing, but for justified and coherent ones. Moreover, we'll have to pay attention to the speaker's other propositional attitudes, such as her desires. For instance, we should be suspicious as to whether we have interpreted the speaker correctly if we attribute to her both the desire to eat a green apple and the belief that this apple is green but no desire to eat this apple. All this is to say that the guiding principle of charity is a principle of rationality. The goal, however, is not to find perfect rationality, but to avoid inexplicable error, or inconsistency, or ignorance. Indeed, as Davidson put it, the goal is not to maximize agreement but to maximize intelligibility. And this is possible only if we assume a modicum of rationality.

According to Davidson, a theory of truth for a language will be correct if not only the formal constraints but also the empirical constraints, that is, the principle of charity in all its complexity, are respected. But just how can the T-sentences be interpretive or meaning giving? How can we replace 'iff' with 'means that'? How can we avoid T-sentences such as '"Snow is white" is true iff grass is green'? For that matter, how can we explain the informative value of a sentence such as 'Phosphorus is Hesperus'? After all, the same object in the world may cause a speaker to utter both 'Phosphorus' and 'Hesperus', so that we may have a T-sentence such as '"Phosphorus is Hesperus" is true iff Phosphorus is Phosphorus', because we have used 'Phosphorus' as the designation of both 'Phosphorus' and 'Hesperus'.

Holism is the heart of the answer to these questions. We can replace 'iff' with 'means that' insofar as, for each T-sentence we may consider as giving the meaning of an object language sentence, we know the axioms of the theory that entail it and we know that it is a theory that meets the formal and empirical constraints. The axioms, to be clear, will eventually be extracted from the T-sentences we'll have come up with. We'll have to observe the speaker use, say, 'Gava' and many other expressions in many different circumstances, and we'll have to test our initial assignments of meaning, for example by prompting the speaker to assent to (or dissent from) our utterance 'Gavagai!' in circumstances where a rabbit is passing by (or a cat is passing by). In short, we'll have to see how 'Gava' systematically contributes to the truth conditions of the sentences in which it occurs; then we'll be in a position to formulate the axiom '"Gava" applies to an object iff the object is a rabbit'. The holistic character of interpretation will prevent us from coming up with T-sentences such as '"Snow is white" is true iff grass is green', most basically because we'll have observed the speaker use 'green' around grass, spinach and green sweaters (among other things) and 'white' around snow, cauliflower and white blouses (among other things). And it will prevent us from coming up with T-sentences such as '"Phosphorus is Hesperus" is true iff Phosphorus is Phosphorus', because such a sentence would be inconsistent with the speaker's believing that Phosphorus is a different planet from Hesperus, for instance. This belief would indicate that she does not mean the same thing by 'Phosphorus' and 'Hesperus', and this is something that should be reflected in our choice of axioms for 'Phosphorus' and 'Hesperus' – we should not use the same name to indicate what they designate.

Given the intricacies involved in respecting the principle of charity, Davidson thought that T-sentences could not be meaning-giving unless we knew the whole language – or at least a good chunk of it, as he came to concede – for which they are T-sentences. This makes the task of the radical interpreter especially daunting, even if at the start we focus just on interpreting very basic sentences uttered in response to objects and events in the environment of speakers and interpreters. But the idea is not actually to embark on radical interpretation. The radical interpretation thought experiment is just that: a thought experiment. Indeed, Davidson never thought that speakers and interpreters actually 'formulate' theories of truth or interpretation. He only thought that reflecting on how they could be formulated would yield an 'important insight' into the nature of meaning. (He even thought that this would yield an insight into how languages are first acquired, as the situation of a first-language learner is in some respects similar to that of a radical interpreter.) For, recall, the ultimate philosophical goal is not to have a theory of interpretation for a speaker. It is not to get clear about how meanings are attributed. It is to get clear about how meanings are constituted. And the claim is that whatever is needed for us to construct a theory of interpretation is also needed for words to mean what they do, and hence to have meaning. What, then, does reflecting on the construction of a theory of interpretation for an alien speaker teach us philosophically about the nature of meaning?

5.3 The lessons of radical interpretation

To begin with, it follows from the thought experiment that meaning is externally determined, that is, determined, at least in part, by features of the environment in which speakers use their words. If what we need to pay attention to in order to interpret a speaker is the features of the environment that we share with her – features that regularly cause her to produce utterances that express beliefs that we, too, are caused to form by those features – then these features play an essential role in determining the meaning of our expressions. Yet it may be said that the thought experiment does not *establish* externalism, as it rests on the assumption that meaning is necessarily public; and this assumption might seem already to presuppose that meaning is necessarily determined by features that are accessible to speakers and their interpreters (we'll come back to this in chapter 7). In spite of this, the thought experiment does shed new light on the externalist answer to the question what determines meaning. To begin with, what is noteworthy is that the externalism that flows from the thought experiment is significantly different from that of Putnam. The connections that are essential to meaning are between states of affairs and events and the (sometimes elliptical) sentences we use to respond to them, not between objects and sub-sentential expressions. In other words, the essential connections are between sentences and what in the world makes them true, not between expressions and what they refer to. Even though, as I said earlier that Davidson conceded, the theory of truth that is to serve as theory of interpretation may not be able to cover all uses of language, it does cover what seems to be the core of language, so that reflecting on how to build it teaches us something about the core of meaning, namely that it is essentially connected to truth.

Another lesson of the thought experiment is that meaning is holistic. There is no question of having specific features of the environment, such as the chemical structure of the liquid referred to by a word, necessarily be the essential determinants of meaning (which is not to say that chemical structure may not play a role in this determination). What the alien speaker's words mean is figured out holistically, on the basis of the many regular uses of her expressions in many different circumstances and the many beliefs she expresses about the particular objects or events she may be responding to with her utterances. And, if what the alien speaker's words mean is figured out holistically, then meaning is also constituted holistically. This is not to say that all of a speaker's uses of words, and hence all her beliefs, are relevant to determining what she means by those words. The belief that rabbits are animals may be central to what a speaker means by 'rabbit', but the belief that rabbits like carrots may not. Davidson does not think that there is a clear line to be drawn between beliefs that are central and beliefs that are not. All we can say is that central beliefs will be those that a speaker would be reluctant to give up (beliefs about chemical structure could be among them). To my mind, however, the most important difference between Putnam's version of externalism and Davidson's is that the latter is not committed to saying that beliefs a speaker is unaware of – other people's beliefs – essentially contribute to what she means by her words. I take this to be an improvement on Putnam's externalism, for, as I said in the previous chapter, it precludes the claim that one often has an incomplete understanding of one's words. But does Davidson's externalism provide a full answer to the question what it is for words to mean what they do? Does reflecting on radical interpretation fulfil Davidson's promise to teach us all there is to know about the nature of meaning? I think not.

5.4   The limits of radical interpretation

Recall that one of Davidson's desiderata was to give an account of meaning that is non-question-begging, that does not presuppose or employ the notion of meaning. He does succeed in doing this insofar as the theorems of the theory of truth that is to serve as a theory of interpretation do not say that a certain sentence has a certain meaning; rather, they say that the sentence has certain truth conditions. And to say that the basic words (the semantical primitives) of the language under study, the object language, contribute to these truth conditions is to say that the axioms for these words are the result of matching a word with some feature of the world – say, 'Phosphorus' with the planet Venus, or 'is a planet' with all objects that are planets. This is to say that each axiom links a basic word with items in the world that contribute to making true the true sentences in which the word occurs. But recall, further, that the truth conditions to be derived from the axioms have to be meaning-giving. As we saw in the previous section, this means that we cannot match a basic word of the language under study with just any word of our own that may be co-referring; for example, we cannot use 'Phosphorus' and 'Hesperus' interchangeably in the axiom for 'Phosphorus' in the object language. We have in effect to be careful and use a word that has the same meaning as the speaker's word – and not just any co-referring word.

What this reveals is that, in building a theory of truth that is to serve as a theory of interpretation, we must draw on evidence that goes beyond the mere connections between the speaker's utterances on the one side and, on the other, objects and events in the environment we share with her. We must draw on knowledge of our own language, on knowledge of what we mean by our words, on knowledge of what beliefs and other propositional attitudes we express by our utterances. But this is to say that the account of meaning afforded by reflecting on radical interpretation, even though the theory of interpretation does not use 'means that' in specifying the speaker's meanings, does end up relying on the notion of meaning, insofar as the interpreter's understanding of her own words plays an essential role in the specification. What she means by her words is part of the evidence she must draw on to come up with proper, that is to say meaning-giving, truth conditions.

This does not take away the positive results of reflecting on radical interpretation. But it may leave dissatisfied those who are seeking a completely reductive account of meaning, one that does not rely at all on the notion of meaning. More on this in the next two chapters.

It is indeed one of the most striking elements of Davidson's enquiry that it is pursued from the point of view of the interpreter – the third-person point of view – thereby resting, as I just stressed, on the interpreter's possession of a language. To attain a fuller account of meaning, we should continue the inquiry and ask how the interpreter herself came to mean what she does by her words. That is, we should continue the inquiry from the point of view of the speaker, the first-person point of view. If the conclusions reached by reflecting on radical interpretation are right, what any language user means by her words depends, at least in part, on features of her environment in response to which she has produced regular utterances. But just how did she come to distinguish among the many aspects of the environment her words may be referring to? Just how did she come to mean *rabbit* by 'rabbit', rather than *fur*, or *fast*, or *cute*? How did she first enter into language? Perhaps, as a result of her responding regularly to features of her environment by perceiving them and acting on them, things got somehow imprinted in her mind or her brain, in such a way that she came to associate words with those internal things, which would thereby constitute the meanings of her words. I have already expressed serious reservations about this idea of association, what I called the associative conception of meaning. Still, I want to turn to the philosopher who most thoroughly attacked it, in part because he argued that this rejection could only lead to scepticism about meaning, the denial of the claim that we ever mean anything by any of our expressions. This is the topic of the next chapter.

References

Davidson, Donald. 2001 [1967]. 'Truth and Meaning', in his *Inquiries into Truth and Interpretation*. Oxford University Press, 17–36.

Davidson, Donald. 2001 [1973]. 'Radical Interpretation', in his *Inquiries into Truth and Interpretation*. Oxford University Press, 125–140.

Further Readings

Davidson's most important sources:

Quine, W. V. O. 1961 [1953]. 'Two Dogmas of Empiricism'. *From a Logical Point of View* (2nd edn). Harvard University Press.

Quine, W. V. O. 2013 [1960]. *Word and Object*. MIT Press. (See esp. ch. 2.)

Tarski, Alfred. 1956 [1936]. 'The Concept of Truth in Formalized Language', translated by J. H. Woodger, in his *Logic, Semantics, Meta-Mathematics*. Oxford University Press, 152–278.

Some of Davidson's early essays in philosophy of language:

Davidson, Donald. 2001. *Inquiries into Truth and Interpretation*. Oxford University Press.

Useful introductions to Davidson's early philosophy of language:

Glüer, Kathrin. 2011. *Donald Davidson: A Short Introduction*. Oxford University Press. (See esp. chs 2 and 3.)

Ramberg, Bjørn T. 1989. *Donald Davidson's Philosophy of Language: An Introduction*. Blackwell.

An important early collection of essays inspired by Davidson's approach to truth and meaning:

Evans, Gareth and John McDowell (eds). 2005 [1976]. *Truth and Meaning: Essays in Semantics*. Oxford University Press.

Important alternative approaches to radical interpretation and theories of meaning:

Lewis, David. 1974. 'Radical Interpretation'. *Synthese*, 27(3/4): 331–344.

Dummett, Michael. 1993 [1974]. 'What Is a Theory of Meaning? (I&II)', in his *The Seas of Language*. Oxford University Press, 1–93.

6

Scepticism about Meaning

I ended the previous chapter by emphasizing a conspicuously missing element in the account of meaning that follows from reflecting on radical interpretation: the point of view of the speaker. It is one thing to adopt the third-person point of view – that of the interpreter – and to project, so to speak, one's language onto that of the speaker to be interpreted. But what is it about us that makes it the case that our use of language is intelligent and not just the product of automatic reactions to the world around us? What is it about us – about our behaviour, or about what goes on inside us – that accounts for our genuinely meaning things by our words, for our using them with genuine understanding? By going outside the mind in search for the source of meaning and by focusing on the world around us, we have to some extent neglected language users themselves. But one would expect them not to be the mere recipients of external causes; one would expect that something about them grounds their intelligent use of language, their using words with understanding.

Stunningly, Saul Kripke, whose earlier work we discussed in chapter 4, argued ten years later that there is in fact nothing about an individual speaker that even constitutes her meaning anything by her words, let alone explains her intelligent use of words. Thus the early 1980s went through what I consider to be another revolution in the history of philosophy of language. What was revolutionary was not only the conclusion Kripke thought he had reached but also the new concerns and issues about meaning that his argument had unveiled, many of which are still subjects of dispute. Prior to Kripke's book, most philosophers held that a proper account of meaning has to be reductive, which is to say that it cannot appeal at all to the notion of meaning in order to explain it. Thanks to Kripke, philosophers started vigorously debating the question whether meaning can really be accounted for in a reductive way and, if not, to what extent anything philosophically constructive can really be said about meaning. They also emphasized for the first time the fact that meaningful expressions must be governed by standards of correct use and asked how we are to conceive of these standards. In particular, they asked whether meaning is in any interesting sense normative, that is, whether using words meaningfully involves any kind of norms that language users ought to follow (besides their using words according to standards of correctness). How, then, to begin with, did Kripke reach the paradoxical conclusion that we never mean anything by any expression? (The conclusion is paradoxical because, on the face of it, if it is right, we cannot say anything, not even that it is right!) As Kripke saw it, it all started with the writings of the later Wittgenstein, in which Kripke found a sceptical challenge that, he thought, could not be met.

6.1 The sceptical challenge

Suppose, to follow Kripke's main example, that you have never computed numbers larger than 57 and that you encounter a 'bizarre' sceptic who challenges your confidence that, when asked to add 68 and 57, you should answer '125'. What makes you so sure, the sceptic asks, that you should not answer '5'? What makes you so sure that by '+' you mean *plus* (addition) rather than *quus* (quaddition) – where 'quus' is defined as a function that yields the sum for numbers lower than 57, and '5 otherwise' – that is, 5 for numbers higher than 57? Kripke focuses on this mathematical example, but the disconcerting sceptical question can be raised for any word of a language. To cite other examples Kripke gives, what makes you so sure that your applying 'table' to the table you see for the first time at the base of the Eiffel Tower is correct? What makes you so sure that by 'table' you mean *table* rather than *tabair*, where 'tabair' is defined as 'anything that is a table not found at the base of the Eiffel Tower, or a chair found there' (Kripke 1982, p. 19)? For that matter, what makes you so sure that your applying 'green' to the golf course you are now walking on is correct? What makes you so sure that by 'green' you mean *green* rather than *grue*, where 'grue' is applied correctly to past objects that were (then) green and to present objects that are (now) blue? (Kripke borrows this famous example from the American philosopher Nelson Goodman.) You may well protest that the sceptic's hypotheses about what you mean are absurd, 'absolutely wild', as Kripke says, that you are utterly convinced that you mean *plus* by '+', *table* by 'table', and *green* by 'green'. But, as the sceptic retorts, she does not doubt your confidence; rather she wants you to tell her what it is about you, about your mind, or about your behaviour that warrants this confidence. Can you point to something about you, a 'fact', as the sceptic calls it, that 'constitutes' your meaning *plus* rather than *quus* by '+', that is, that makes it the case that it is *plus* that you mean by '+' (to stick with the main example)? Indeed, can you point to a fact about you that justifies your answering '125' when asked to add 68 and 57?

These two questions, one formulated in terms of constitution, the other in terms of justification, indicate that the sceptical challenge is twofold: not only is the sceptic seeking a fact about you that makes it true that you mean what you do by your word, namely that by '+' you mean *plus* rather than *quus*; this fact must also justify your using the word in the way you do, namely your answering '125' rather than '5' when queried '68 + 57 equals what?' Thus it is a fact to which you must somehow have access. As we'll see soon in more detail, these two parts of the challenge are related to two of the conditions that, I said in chapter 2, must at least be made room for in any acceptable account of meaning. The constitutive question is linked to the idea that meaningful words are governed by standards of correct application; meaning-constituting facts are supposed to provide these standards, that is, be usable as standards in light of which any application of a word can be deemed to be correct or incorrect. For instance, the meaning-constituting fact for 'green' would provide the standard that determines that 'green' is applied correctly to grass and incorrectly to snow. The justificatory question is linked to the idea that the meaningful use of words is intelligent or intentional, the product of understanding, something associated with the language user rather than a 'jack-in-the-box' response (to use Kripke's term), the product of luck, something arbitrary and dissociated from the language user. Thus one could appeal to such a meaning-constituting fact to justify one's answering '125' when asked to add 68 and 57. Kripke's sceptic argues that no such individual facts are to be found. How does she do this?

6.2   The sceptical argument

There are several candidate facts that Kripke considers and rejects, the most important of which are as follows.

To keep with Kripke's main example, first there is the fact that in the past I have used '+' in a certain way: for the most part I came up with the sum when asked to add numbers (I may occasionally have made a mistake). But the number of additions I have performed is of course limited. As a matter of fact, as we are supposing, I have never added numbers larger than 57. If so, the way I have used '+' in the past is compatible with my meaning *quus* rather than *plus* by '+'; given the numbers I added, I would have come up with the sum in the past even if I meant *quus* by '+' (sum and quum would be indistinguishable for those numbers). Of course, this compatibility would not be present if my past use of '+' somehow involved my meaning *plus* by '+'. But my past use is just that: a series of bodily movements, the regular uttering of sounds in response to, say, queries that are themselves utterings of sounds. Once we acknowledge what kind of phenomenon the mere use of words is, the question becomes: what is it about my past use of '+' that makes it the case that I mean *plus* rather than *quus* by '+'? I could take it to express that meaning, but on the face of it I could also take it to express the meaning of *quus*. Distressingly, as I see it, whenever and however I use '+', I could, on the basis of my past use, take '+' to have a meaning such that my present use is correct. This is distressing, for it amounts to saying that I do not in fact mean anything by '+', because words whose uses can be deemed to be correct no matter what simply do not mean anything. Thus the view that past uses constitute the meaning of our words in fact leads to scepticism about meaning, in the devastating sense that the possibility of meaning is being denied.

The second, perhaps equally obvious candidate as a meaning-constituting fact is that I have internalized instructions about how to use '+'. My present answer to the query '68 + 57 = ?' is based on these instructions, which cover cases that go beyond what I have done so far, and not on the finite set of additions I have performed. The problem here, the sceptic responds, has to do with the meaning of the instructions I have given myself. Let us say, as would be very plausible, that these instructions contain the word 'count'. So, to follow Kripke's suggestion, to add x and y is to take, say, a bunch of marbles, count x marbles in one bunch, count y marbles in another, put the two bunches together, count the marbles in the combined bunch, and declare the result to be x + y. As might be expected, the sceptic now challenges my confidence that by 'count' I mean *count* rather than *quount*, where to quount is to count, unless what is counted is the union of two bunches of items one of which contains 57 or more of them – in which case the answer should be '5'. In short, the problem with this candidate fact is that, whatever instructions I may think of, they are open to various interpretations. It is only if I take them to have a certain meaning that they can determine what the correct use of '+' is. Actually, as I see it again, the most fundamental problem is that, regardless of how I answer the query, be it with '125' or '5' or whatnot, I could always take these instructions in such a way that my use is correct. But, again, a word that can always be said to be used correctly regardless of how it is used cannot mean *plus*, or *quus*, or anything for that matter.

The third candidate fact – that of having a mental image – will remind us of Locke. Let us use here the example of 'green', as it is hard to fathom what mental image we could associate with '+'. The idea is that, whenever I use 'green', I form a certain image in my mind that constitutes my meaning *green* by 'green' and guides my applications of 'green'. If I want my application to be correct, I apply 'green' to grass; if not, I apply it to snow. In each case, I check my application against the image in my mind, which provides the standard that determines the correctness or incorrectness of my application. There are two problems with this candidate fact, both of which I mentioned when we discussed

Locke. First, I do not need to have an image in my mind in order to mean *green* by 'green'. Second, the image in my mind may not be sufficient for me to mean *green* by 'green'. What is the image in my mind supposed to look like for it to count – and for me to take it – as providing the standard of correctness for my applications of 'green' rather than 'leaf', or 'shape', or . . .? After all, no image could be such that it was only of green; it would have to have other properties as well. But then, if I take it as an image of green, it may count as providing the standard of correctness for my applications of 'green'. If I take it as an image of a leaf, it may count as providing the standard for my applications of 'leaf'. If I take it as an image of a shape, it may count as providing the standard for my applications of 'shape'. But how is it established how I should take it? It looks as if it is open to me to take it one way or another; indeed, no matter how I apply 'green', it looks as if it is open to me always to take it in such a way that my application is correct. Thus I apply 'green' correctly to the golf course if I take my image to be that of green. I apply 'green' correctly to the tree leaves (no matter their colour) if I take my image to be that of leaf. I apply 'green' correctly to the sample of shape (no matter its colour) if I take my image to be that of shape – and so on and so forth. But if 'green' is applied correctly no matter how it is used, 'green' does not mean *green* – or, for that matter, *leaf*, or *shape*. It does not mean anything, which shows that this view about what it is for words to have meaning again leads in fact to scepticism about meaning.

The fourth candidate fact – that of grasping a sense – will remind us of Frege. Senses, you will recall, are supposed to be abstract entities. This immediately makes this proposal harder to understand than the previous one. For we may understand what it is to have a mental image and to associate it with a word – we sometimes do that. But it is harder to understand what it is to grasp an abstract entity and to associate it with a word. This makes it harder to point to cases where I clearly do mean something by a word but do not associate a sense with it. Still, the problems with this fourth candidate are in some ways similar to the previous problems. First, it is hard to believe that I need to grasp a sense in order to mean *green* by 'green'. Second and more importantly, what makes it the case that the sense I associate with 'green' is greenness? Assuming that there are senses such as greenness, leafness, shape, and so on, how do I get to match, so to speak, my words with them? Again, I may apply 'green' correctly to the golf course because I take the sense I associate with 'green' to be greenness. Again, I may apply 'green' correctly to the tree leaves (no matter their colour) because I take the sense I associate with 'green' to be leafness. Again, I may apply 'green' correctly to the sample of shape (no matter its colour) because I take the sense I associate with 'green' to be shape – and so on. But again, if 'green' is applied correctly no matter how it is used, 'green' does not mean *green*, or *leaf*, or *shape* – or indeed anything. Again, scepticism about meaning follows from this view.

The fifth candidate fact is readily dismissed by Kripke, though, interestingly, he also admits that, properly understood, it may be 'irrefutable'. The suggestion here is this: what constitutes my meaning what I do by a word is, quite simply, the 'primitive state' of my meaning what I do. To mean *plus* by '+' is simply to be in the primitive state of meaning *plus* by '+'. Kripke rejects the proposal first on the ground that it is 'completely mysterious' what kind of state this 'primitive state' is supposed to be. Second, he does not think that this state could really constitute meaning; for it would have to be, as he puts it, 'a finite object, contained in our finite minds'. Therefore it could not encompass the infinite number of ways in which I might apply a word; indeed, given its finiteness, it could always be interpreted in a deviant way. For instance, the alleged primitive state of someone's meaning *plus* by '+' could, after all, be interpreted in a quus-like way. To my mind, however, there is something puzzling about Kripke's diagnosis here. For, if the primitive state is genuinely a state of meaning something by a word, it should encompass all possible applications of the word whose meaning it constitutes. It should not need interpretation. We'll come back to this in the next chapter, when we consider a more developed non-reductive account of meaning.

The sixth candidate fact seems to be the most promising, and it is the one to which Kripke devotes most of his attention (it was hardly discussed by Wittgenstein himself, but by the time of Kripke's writing it had become, and still is, one of the prominent candidates). Recall that part of the problem with past uses is the finiteness of the uses on which my present application is supposed to be based. This leaves open the compatibility of various applications, all of which could be said to be correct. To deal with this predicament, however, instead of past uses, we could have *dispositions* to use be the relevant meaning-constituting facts. Thus, in the case of '+', the relevant fact would be my disposition to answer any query of the form '$x + y = ?$' with the sum. In the case of 'green', the relevant fact would be my disposition to apply 'green' to green things. On the face of it, the dispositional view looks like a vast improvement on the past use view, precisely because dispositions cover not merely past uses but all future and all possible uses. My past use of '+' is compatible with both my meaning *plus* and my meaning *quus* by '+'. Prima facie at least, my disposition to use '+' in certain ways is not so compatible. My past use of 'green' is compatible with both my meaning *green* and my meaning *grue* by 'green'. Again, prima facie at least, my disposition to use 'green' in certain ways is not so compatible. But which ways exactly? Can we characterize the relevant disposition so that the meaning of the word it is supposed to constitute is indeed determinate? And can we do this in a non-question-begging way, that is, without involving the notion of meaning in our characterization?

A disposition, as it is thought of in this context, is a physical state, a state of the brain, which no more wears a meaning on its sleeve, as it were, than a past use, or a set of instructions, or a mental image, or an abstract entity. So what makes a disposition the disposition that it is? And this is to ask: what makes it the meaning-constituting fact that it is supposed to be? Of course, we do not have access to dispositions in the way we may have access to mental images or other states of the mind. For this reason, some have thought that the question of interpretation, of how to take the disposition, does not arise. Still, presumably there must be a way to characterize the disposition that is supposed to constitute, say, my meaning *green* by 'green'. The difficulty is that the characterization has to cover all the possible cases of my using 'green' correctly, where this includes cases that differ from any I have encountered or conceived of so far, and it has to exclude all the possible cases of my using 'green' incorrectly (of course as I still mean *green* by 'green', as when I wish to misrepresent snow). And, to repeat, the characterization cannot involve the notion of meaning (it cannot be in semantic terms, as I will sometimes put it in what follows). Thus I cannot characterize the disposition that is supposed to constitute my meaning *green* by 'green' as the disposition to use 'green' to *mean green*, or to *talk about* what is green. It is true that I have this disposition, but acknowledging this is not terribly enlightening (unless perhaps more is said about this use, which we'll do in the next chapter). So which is the disposition that constitutes my meaning what I do by a word? This question is also raised by Kripke in connection with two related concerns he has about the dispositional view.

First, dispositions are finite. To go back to Kripke's main example, it is not true that I will respond with the sum when queried about the sum of any two numbers, for some pairs of numbers are too large for my mind or brain to grasp. Second, I am also disposed to make mistakes; indeed, I am not always disposed to use an expression in the correct way. The usual reply to these worries is that dispositions come with what is called *ceteris paribus* or 'all things being equal' clauses. Thus I would come up with the sum when asked to add very large numbers – if I had enough brain matter, if I could live long enough, and so on. I would apply 'green' to green things provided I was not tired, or drunk, or distracted, or . . . unless I wanted to joke, or lie, or mislead my audience, and so on. Kripke does consider these replies and rejects them, for reasons I take to be related to the worry I expressed above.

The question is, how are we to characterize the relevant *ceteris paribus* clauses? Kripke thinks that this cannot be done without invoking the notion of meaning – specifically, without assuming the meaning-constituting fact whose existence the sceptic is calling into question. To start with the problem of finiteness, Kripke asks: how am I to tell how I would behave under idealized conditions? How am I to tell what I would do if I were given extra brain power or some life-prolonging elixir? I may become insane or a deviant language user. What, then, can I offer as a characterization of what I would do, apart from saying that I would conform to my present intentions to behave as I always have? Thus, if I were given the means to compute large numbers, I would come up with the sum, when queried 'x + y = ?' for some presently unmanageable x and y. But this presupposes that I intend to mean *plus* by '+', and thus that there is, after all, a fact as to what I mean – which is precisely what the sceptic is calling into question and asking that I characterize in such a way that it does ground my meaning *plus* by '+' without simply presupposing that it does. That I have such meaning intentions may well be true but, again, acknowledging this sheds little

light on what it is for words to mean what they do;
for the explanation is circular: it says, in effect, that to
mean something by a word is to be disposed to use it
to mean what it does. The same problem arises if we
try to characterize the disposition in such a way that
mistakes are excluded. Thus I might characterize the
disposition that constitutes my meaning *plus* by '+' as
the disposition I would have if all my dispositions to
make mistakes were removed. But how do I characterize
this latter disposition? It is just the disposition I would
have if I did not have the dispositions to give answers
that conflict with the correct applications dictated by
what I meant. The circularity of the response is again
apparent, as it takes for granted that there is a fact as to
what I mean by '+' but does not succeed in characterizing
it in non-semantic terms.

The foregoing discussion suggests that dispositions
also fail as candidate facts that constitute what we mean
by our words. Even if we do have dispositions to use
words in certain ways, as long as we think of them in
reductive terms, that is, in physical or behaviouristic
rather than semantic terms, it is indeterminate which
dispositions constitute which meanings. It is not that
they have to be taken or interpreted in certain ways in
order to constitute meanings, as do the other candidate
facts we considered. It is that any characterization
we can think of, insofar as we can think of one, is
compatible with our meaning different things by the
word whose meaning the disposition is supposed to
constitute. Moreover, as I mentioned earlier, we have
no access to the brain states that our dispositions are
supposed to be. This leads to Kripke's final blow to the
dispositional view.

Kripke's last objection is connected to the second
part of the sceptical challenge, which demands that the
meaning-constituting facts justify our using words the
way we do; and thus, as I said earlier, it is connected to the
demand that our account of meaning at least make room

for the distinction between behaviour that is intelligent or intentional and behaviour that is not. The objection is, on the surface, quite straightforward. According to Kripke, the main problem with the dispositional view is that dispositions have no prescriptive power. They do not entail that words *should* be used in certain ways, only that they *will* be used in certain ways. Thus, from the fact that my meaning *plus* by '+' is my being disposed to come up with the sum when queried 'x + y = ?', it may follow that I *will* answer '125' when asked '68 + 57 = ?'; it does not follow that I *should* come up with that answer. But my meaning what I do by an expression does entail that I should use it in certain ways, not that I will use it in certain ways. As Kripke puts it, the connection between meaning and use is normative, not descriptive.

The claim that meaning is normative may have caused more ink to be spilled than any other claim Kripke made in his book on Wittgenstein. This is in part because, on second thought, the claim is not all that clear. For one thing, does my meaning what I do by an expression oblige me, categorically, to use it correctly? For instance, if I mean *green* by 'green', do I have the (at least prima facie) categorical obligation to apply it only to green things (where this obligation is semantic, stemming purely from what I mean, and not merely, say, moral, requiring me to tell the truth)? Or does my meaning *green* by 'green' oblige me to use it in certain ways, correctly or incorrectly, only depending on what I want to achieve by using it, in which case the obligation is just hypothetical? For instance, if I want to tell the truth, I should describe the green blouse as green; if I want to mislead my interlocutor, I should describe the red blouse as green. But I shall not enter the controversy surrounding these questions, as I think that the claim that meaning is normative can also be understood in a rather uncontroversial way.

As I see it, the claim is connected to the idea that language use is intelligent or intentional, because for language use to be so requires that, when we use words meaningfully, we have an understanding of what we are doing, which involves understanding that what we are doing may be correct or incorrect. Thus I use 'green' to describe the green blouse because I want my description to be correct. I use 'green' to describe the red blouse because I want my description to be incorrect. Acknowledging a meaning-constituting fact provides us with a reason, which we may appeal to in order to justify our use. In each case, I used 'green' because I know what I mean by 'green', and hence I know what it is to use it accordingly – correctly or incorrectly, as the case may be (which does not entail that I always know whether my use is in fact correct; sometimes I do not, as when I say 'Jim is wearing a green shirt today' but may be wrong as I have not seen Jim). Thus the meaning-constituting fact is one that we must not only be connected to – it cannot just happen to belong to us – but be connected to in a special way. For it is a fact that in part guides the applications of our words and in part tells us which ones are to be deemed correct and which ones are not. (I say 'in part' because the world itself, both inside and outside us, also dictates our applications; for example, I should say 'Jim is wearing a green shirt' if I want to tell the truth (what is inside me) and if Jim is wearing a green shirt (what is outside me).) This talk of guidance or telling does not have to be taken literally, however. To say that the fact is guiding the uses of our words, telling us how to classify them as correct or incorrect, is only to say that we recognize it for what it is, as calling for certain uses and assessments rather than others and thereby making our behaviour intelligent or intentional rather than robotic or automatic.

If all this is right, it is not just that dispositions cannot meet the second part of the challenge; the claim that they cannot meet the first part either is reinforced. For if dispositions are the wrong kind of fact, in that they cannot be summoned to justify our uses of words, and if meaning-constituting facts must play this justificatory role, then meaning-constituting facts cannot be dispositions. To insist that dispositions could still be meaning-constituting insofar as they could still, mysteriously, underwrite the distinction between correct and incorrect applications of expressions, thereby meeting the first part of the sceptical challenge, would appear to reduce language users to mere automata. To avoid this and allow language use to be intelligent or intentional, we need not only a fact that can provide standards of application but a fact of which language users can be aware. If Kripke, on behalf of the sceptic, is right, there are no such facts to be found. And, if so, according to the sceptic, we never mean anything by any of our expressions.

But we do! (Please, keep reading!) So, how are we to proceed to show that we do?

6.3   Addressing the sceptic

There are three options. Either, first, we find a kind of fact that Kripke has failed to consider or failed to consider properly; or, second, we concede to the sceptic that there is no meaning-constituting fact of any kind to be found and we figure out a different way to explain our ascriptions of meaning to utterances; or, third, we argue that the sceptic's conception of what it is for words to have meaning is misguided and therefore the sceptical problem is unmotivated.

Kripke called the first option a 'straight solution', on the grounds that it provides the sceptic with the kind of fact she was seeking. This option has been quite popular, not in that a candidate fact has been discovered that Kripke had neglected, but in that several attempts have been made to defend a dispositionalist – and thus reductive – account of meaning. I shall not review them here but, in any case, in light of Kripke's arguments, it seems to me that, insofar as the fact that the sceptic is looking for is a reductive fact, a fact that wears no meaning on its sleeve, no such fact is to be found. Semantic non-reductionism seems to be one of the main conclusions of the sceptical argument and has indeed also been endorsed by many philosophers. Not all the candidate facts considered were reductive facts, however. In particular, it might be thought that grasping a sense is a semantic fact par excellence. Senses are supposed to be meanings. But we saw that the view that grasping a sense is the relevant kind of meaning-constituting fact faces the indeterminacy problem all the same. What is less obvious, notwithstanding Kripke's diagnosis, is whether the view that meaning-constituting facts are just primitive states of meaning also faces that problem. I shall return to this in the next chapter. For now, let us examine Kripke's own solution; for there has to be one, even for the sceptic. We must somehow make sense of what we do when we are attributing meaning to people's words.

6.4 A sceptical solution to the sceptical problem

Kripke provides what he calls a 'sceptical solution'. What makes the sceptical solution *sceptical* is that it agrees with the sceptic that there is no fact about an individual that constitutes her meaning what she does by any expression. It concedes to the sceptic that ascriptions of meaning such as 'Jones means *plus* by "+"' have no truth conditions insofar as no individual facts could make them true. What makes the sceptical solution a *solution* is that it provides us with a way of justifying our ascriptions of meaning to people's utterances, though not on the kind of grounds the sceptic sought and revealed to be unattainable. Thus, according to Kripke, though ascriptions of meaning have no truth conditions, they do have 'assertibility' or 'justification' conditions, that is, conditions under which they are justifiably asserted. Therefore, to solve the sceptical problem, we have to ask, not what must be the case for ascriptions of meaning to be true, but what the circumstances are under which ascriptions of meaning are appropriately made. Moreover, we have to ask what is the role and utility in our lives of making such ascriptions. It then turns out that ascriptions of meaning to an individual's utterances are justified if the individual's applications of words agree often enough with those made by the members of the linguistic community that is considering her. Thus, if Jones answers often enough a query of the form 'x + y = ?' with the sum, we are justified in saying that he means *plus* by '+'. Jones himself is entitled to say this, since he has the inclination to give answers that conform to ours. The utility of this practice is evident, as it allows individuals to communicate with one another and get their wishes fulfilled.

Importantly, the sceptical solution yields a social view of meaning, as it involves essential reference to a community. Although to mean what one does by an expression is, in the end, to have an inclination to use that expression in certain ways on certain occasions – an inclination that, Kripke declares, is 'primitive', not to be further elucidated – this inclination has to be legitimized by others. It cannot be the case that whatever application seems to an individual to be correct is correct; this would annihilate the distinction between correctness and incorrectness – which has to be objective, that is, independent of what any language user takes it to be (my deeming my application of 'flat' to be correct when I utter 'The earth is flat' does not make it correct) – and hence it would annihilate meaning. Rather, the meanings we ascribe to an individual's utterances and, thus, the ways in which we distinguish between correct and incorrect applications of her words essentially depend on the meanings, and thus the standards of application, that the community considering her ascribes to its words. (Note that the community's practices of using words in certain ways do not provide its members' utterances with truth conditions. There is still nothing that could make them true; in particular, the community's dispositions to use words in certain ways cannot constitute the required facts, as they are subject to the sceptical challenge as much as individual dispositions are.)

These are the bare bones of Kripke's sceptical solution. How satisfactory is it?

It has in fact been widely criticized, not least because it is hard to be convinced that meaning has been retrieved after having been so blatantly renounced. Still, in line with the narrative we have followed throughout the chapters, let us ask whether the solution meets the two conditions on an acceptable account of meaning that I associated with the two parts of the sceptical challenge. Of course, these two conditions cannot be met by appealing to meaning-constituting facts, since the sceptic has denied their existence. But it seems to me that a sceptic intent on solving the sceptical problem, albeit sceptically, still owes us an account of what underwrites our distinguishing between correct and incorrect applications of words and between intelligent and automatic linguistic behaviour. On the surface, Kripke seems to have provided that.

First, we can distinguish between correct and incorrect applications of an individual's words by appealing to the standards at play in the community that is considering her. Kripke leaves it unclear just how to determine which community it is that is considering her (a problem for his solution, but one that I shall not pursue here). Still, second, since, on the most plausible scenario, which is often endorsed by Kripke, her language use is the result of training by her community fellows into a practice of using words in certain ways, it is reasonable to think that she would thereby have acquired an understanding of what she is doing, and thus that her behaviour is intelligent. The assumption would be that she has been trained in a community of people who exhibit understanding of what they are doing – not in that they can provide the kind of justification the sceptic sought, but in that they know how to make the relevant distinctions – and have inculcated this understanding in her. But this twofold answer is good only as far as it goes.

As has often been pointed out, presumably we do not want to say that whatever seems to an entire community to be the correct application of a word is the correct application (all members of a community deeming their application of 'flat' to be correct in the utterance 'The earth is flat' does not make it correct). We can accept that it is a community, rather than single individuals, that sets the standards of application that govern the use of their words. But, once these standards are set, it is not up to the community to say that they are met or not on any given occasion of use. One question is, then, how are those standards set to begin with, such that they can indeed be respected or not objectively? Second, just how did the members of a community get to have an understanding of what they are doing? We still have no clue as to how to answer these questions. Perhaps this was to be expected. Perhaps these questions are, after all, misguided. If no facts make ascriptions of meaning true, if no facts ground the distinction between correct and incorrect applications, we should not be looking beyond the mere 'brute' agreement that underlies our fruitful practices of using words in certain ways. We should remain quiet about this.

But can we not do better?

6.5   A dissolution of the sceptical problem

Mercifully, as some would think, there is a third way, not envisaged by Kripke, to address the sceptical problem, namely to dissolve it by showing that it rests on mistaken premises – specifically, on an incoherent conception of what it is to mean something by one's words.

Recall that the sceptic is looking for something about the individual speaker that makes her use of words meaningful. In effect, the sceptic is asking the question I mentioned at the beginning of the third chapter, about what must be added to dead signs for them to become alive and thus meaningful. And the sceptic is pursuing one of the two paths that, I suggested, could initially be taken, namely that of looking at the individual's mind, or brain, or behaviour, to see whether she can find something there with which signs could be connected or associated (this is a version of what I call the associative conception of meaning). And the sceptic finds nothing. But what does not seem to occur to her is that her finding nothing, rather than forcing her to conclude that there are no meaning facts, is an indication that something in her approach has gone wrong. Perhaps words do not get meaning simply by being associated with facts or entities of one kind or another. Perhaps words get meaning in some other, more complicated way.

What has gone wrong is, at bottom, quite blatant. All the candidate meaning-constituting facts that Kripke, following Wittgenstein, has considered are such that they could do their constituting job only if they were taken in certain ways. However, in order to take them in certain ways, one needs a language. One needs a language to be able to take one's past uses of '+', or instructions for its use, to constitute one's meaning *plus* rather than *quus*. One needs a language to be able to take a mental image, or a sense grasped by the mind, to constitute one's meaning *green* rather than *grue* by 'green'. What this suggests is that the sceptic's demand, rather than being unmeetable, is simply incoherent, as one needs a language in order to be able to identify what is supposed to provide one's words with meaning to begin with. As for dispositions, they are in a way worse off than the other candidate facts, as we do not have access to them and so, strictly speaking, could not associate our words with them. Of course, we have access to the behaviour that may be said to be caused by our dispositions. But the same behaviour is compatible with a variety of dispositions; my coming up with the sum when asked 'x + y = ?' for any numbers lower than 57 is compatible with my being disposed to come up with either the sum or the quum.

If the foregoing is right, then there is no sceptical problem that needs to be solved. Rather, the problem has been dissolved. We are, however, left with no account of meaning. Some philosophers, taking themselves to follow Wittgenstein, have maintained that the right conclusion to draw from the sceptic's considerations is that no account of meaning is forthcoming. According to this line of thought, it may be fruitful to describe language use, to show the many ways in which, as a matter of fact, we do use words meaningfully, but the foundational question what makes meaning possible cannot be answered. No account is even needed, since there is no problem about meaning to be solved. In fact, for these philosophers, semantic non-reductionism, the view that an account of meaning that does not rely on the notion of meaning cannot be obtained, entails semantic quietism, the view that nothing philosophically illuminating can be said about meaning. Others, however – and some of these also take themselves to follow Wittgenstein – believe that non-reductionism is not the end of our philosophical enquiry; it is compatible with constructive philosophical work. What these two groups have in common is their rejecting the sceptic's challenge as ungrounded and their consequently answering Wittgenstein's call to pay closer attention to how people use their words. This is what I do in the next and final chapter.

References

Kripke, Saul. 1982. *Wittgenstein on Rules and Private Language*. Harvard University Press.
Wittgenstein, Ludwig. 2009 [1953]. *Philosophical Investigations* (4th edn), edited by P. M. S. Hacker and Joachim Schulte, translated by G. E. M. Anscombe, P. M. S. Hacker, and Joachim Schulte. Wiley Blackwell.

Further Readings

Two excellent collections of articles on semantic scepticism:
Miller, Alexander and Crispin Wright (eds). 2002. *Rule-Following and Meaning*. McGill-Queen's.
Verheggen, Claudine (ed.). 2024. *Kripke's* Wittgenstein on Rules and Private Language *at 40*. Cambridge University Press.

In these collections, see in particular:
- on the nature of the sceptical problem: essays by Paul Boghossian and John McDowell in Miller and Wright, 2002 and essays by Alexander Miller and Hannah Ginsborg in Verheggen, 2024;
- on constructive readings of Kripke's sceptical solution: essays by Arif Ahmed and Christopher Campbell in Verheggen, 2024;
- for various straight solutions to the sceptical problem: essays by Simon Blackburn, Paul Horwich, and Ruth Garrett Millikan in Miller and Wright, 2002 and essays by Henry Jackman and James Shaw in Verheggen, 2024;
- on a constructive non-reductive response to the sceptic: essays by Olivia Sultanescu and Claudine Verheggen in Verheggen, 2024.

Dispositionalist responses to the sceptical problem:
Ginet, Carl. 1992. 'The Dispositionalist Solution to Wittgenstein's Problem about Understanding a Rule:

Answering Kripke's Objections'. *Midwest Studies in Philosophy*, 17(1): 53–73.

Horwich, Paul. 1998. *Meaning*. Oxford University Press.

Martin, C. B. and John Heil. 1998. 'Rules and Powers'. *Noûs*, 32(S12): 283–312.

Warren, Jared. 2020. 'Killing Kripkenstein's Monster'. *Noûs*, 54(2): 257–89.

Various takes on semantic normativity:

Ginsborg, Hannah. 2011. 'Primitive Normativity and Skepticism about Rules'. *Journal of Philosophy*, 108(5): 227–254.

Glüer, Kathrin and Åsa Wikforss. 2009. 'Against Content Normativity'. *Mind*, 118(469): 31–70.

Verheggen, Claudine. 2011. 'Semantic Normativity and Naturalism'. *Logique et Analyse*, 54(216): 553–567.

Whiting, Daniel. 2009. 'Is Meaning Fraught with Ought?' *Pacific Philosophical Quarterly*, 90(4): 535–555.

7

Meaning and Use

Let us start by taking stock of the progress we have made so far towards answering the question what it is for words to mean what they do. Partly in light of the difficulties we encountered in looking inside language users' minds to answer this question, we turned our attention in chapter 4 to the external items – objects of all kinds and properties thereof – that words are about. Although externalizing meaning in this way is promising, we had to conclude that the accounts on offer are incomplete at best. We were still missing an explanation of just how the connections between words and those items are established. Even if the accounts provided some understanding of how *some* such connections may be established, the explanation relied on taking for granted that some words are already endowed with meaning and hence can be used to introduce connections between other words and their referents, as in 'This liquid is called "water".' As we saw in the case of general terms, even this explanation was troublesome, for it did not seem to do justice to what it is that people do when they succeed in communicating with one another. Accordingly, we turned to a different kind of connection between words and world: the connection between sentences and the events and states of affairs they are about. And we scrutinized these connections by asking how people may understand other speakers from scratch. This inquiry, however, was conducted from the third-person point of view, the point of view of the radical interpreter, who, perforce, has a language. Consequently we seemed to lose track of speakers themselves, of how they, from the first-person point of view, come to mean what they do by their words and what it is about them that makes their language use intelligent or intentional rather than the mere product of external causes. This, in turn, led us to investigate anew language users themselves, their minds and their behaviour, to see whether something about them could after all explain their meaning what they do and their doing so in an intelligent way. And we were left with little explanation. Insofar as people can be said to mean anything by their words, it is because they use them in ways that conform to how members of the community that is considering them – or, more plausibly, the community they belong to – use them. But we were left in the dark as to how these community practices themselves come about. This, we surmised, would be as it should be, if Kripke was correct in denying that ascriptions of meaning are ever true.

This denial was in part based on the conclusion that we cannot account for the meaning of words simply by appealing to entities or facts that are themselves devoid of meaning and, more generally, by expecting that words owe their meaning simply to their being associated with entities or facts of one kind or another. And we ended up suggesting that this associative conception of meaning should be rejected, which in turn prompted us to continue the inquiry. For there is in fact something we have not yet investigated properly. So far, we have been going back and forth between considering language users on the one hand and what they use their words to talk about on the other. We have focused on one or the other side of the connection, without giving proper attention to the connection itself, that is, to language *in* use. We looked at this a bit when we discussed radical interpretation, but reflecting on radical interpretation did not deliver an account of the exact ways language users' uses of words get to be about non-linguistic reality – specifically, as I mentioned at the end of chapter 5, of how they manage to latch onto specific aspects of this reality. This, as I put it, is because in radical interpretation we focus on the third-person point of view. In this chapter we'll examine an account of meaning that incorporates the first-person point of view. This account, though non-reductive, is a constructive account: it does shed light on the nature of meaning. But, as already mentioned, there are those who think that adopting non-reductionism is tantamount to adopting quietism, to abandoning any hope of illuminating philosophically the nature of meaning. According to them, examining language in use yields no constructive claims about how meaning is possible but only descriptive claims about how meaning is actual. I start by examining this position.

7.1 Quietism about meaning

It may be thought that we have already paid sufficient attention to use when we considered past uses of words and dispositions to use words in certain ways as possible determinants of meaning. But the quietist's suggestion is not that we examine uses that are mere bodily movements – utterings of sounds, themselves caused perhaps by brain states. The suggestion is that we think of language uses as uses of words to mean certain things or, to return to the metaphor, as uses that are alive. This quietism, as we saw, is motivated by the realisation that there is no sceptical problem to be solved after all. And, the quietist line of thought continues, if there is no problem to be solved, there is no constructive work to be done. Specifically, for the quietist, there is no problem that motivates the question how meaning is possible. If the sceptic's associative conception of meaning were acceptable, it would prompt such a question – how could adding something to a dead sign make it meaningful? The sceptic, reasonably, thought that it could not; she went on to conclude that meaning is not actual and to look for a different explanation of our ascriptions of meaning. However, if the problem is based on an erroneous conception of what it is for words to have meaning, the problem disappears. Stop thinking of signs as dead, and pay attention to how they are alive in use. Is there a problem there? There is not. The meaningful use of language is just as transparent a fact of life as are the facts that we walk, eat, drink, and play. This is not to say that we are always clear about any particular use of language or that the meaning of a word always lies on the surface of its use, so to speak, as Wittgenstein abundantly illustrated.

Take the word 'game', for instance – one of Wittgenstein's famous examples. We use it to talk about board games, card games, ball games, Olympic games, and so on. What do all these uses have in common? Not anything in particular, Wittgenstein (2009: §66) answers, but 'a complicated network of similarities overlapping and criss-crossing'. Wittgenstein calls these similarities 'family resemblances', as they are akin to the similarities that overlap and criss-cross among the members of a family: build, features, colour of eyes, gait, temperament, and so on. Or take the name 'Moses', another of Wittgenstein's examples. What does one mean if one says 'Moses did not exist?' Whom is one talking about? Following Russell, Wittgenstein answers, it could be the man who led the Israelites through the wilderness or the man who, as a child, was taken out of the Nile by Pharaoh's daughter. But one could also mean to talk about the man who did a good deal of what the Bible relates of Moses. However, Wittgenstein asks, how many of those deeds? Does this question need to be answered in order to communicate using 'Moses'? Does a name need to have a fixed meaning in order to be used meaningfully? Wittgenstein's answer is that it need not. It is important to note, however, as will soon become relevant, that not having a fixed meaning, as I take Wittgenstein to understand this claim, is not tantamount to not being governed by a standard of correct use. I take his point to be that, both in the case of family resemblance terms and in the case of ordinary proper names, no set of necessary and sufficient conditions for their correct use can be given. Consequently, in neither case can the standards that govern the terms' use be specified without drawing on their meaning. Thus, if 'game' means *game*, then 'game' is applied correctly to all things that are games and only to them; if 'Moses' means *Moses*, then 'Moses' is applied correctly to Moses and only to Moses.

The moral of the above remarks is that, if you want to learn something about language, just pay close attention to the multifarious ways in which we use it and communicate with it. Indeed, pay attention to how we use it, not just to describe states of affairs and states of mind, but to give orders, ask questions, tell jokes, curse, greet, and so on, to mention some of the uses listed by Wittgenstein. Then you will learn something about how language functions. So far, so quietist. No constructive work is to be accomplished, no theory of what it is for words to have meaning is to be advanced. For a word to have meaning is simply for it to be used in a language (where at least some words must be used on several occasions), but uses are too diverse and complex to be regimented into any instructive categories; all we can do is describe them.

This quietist interpretation is the most widespread interpretation of Wittgenstein. But Wittgenstein also makes remarks that could be construed as not merely descriptive, and thus as encouraging non-quietism.

7.2   Towards non-quietism

Two of Wittgenstein's remarks are particularly noteworthy.

First, Wittgenstein insists that language use rests on agreement, not just in definitions, but in judgements. This insistence could of course be based on a survey of language use, and thus could be tantamount to a merely descriptive remark. But I think that other considerations may also be grounding it, thereby inviting a non-quietist construal. This is in part because the insistence that agreement in definitions and judgements is needed could be taken to concern not just the possibility of communication but the very possibility of language as well. Thus we must agree about the meaning of the words we use, about how we define them when a definition is called for, and we must do so not just in order to communicate – for it goes without saying that if a speaker and a hearer do not assign the same meanings to the speaker's words, they cannot communicate. In addition, according to this interpretation of Wittgenstein, a speaker must have reached some agreement with other speakers on what they mean by at least some of their words in order to mean anything by any word at all. This latter statement does not sound like a merely descriptive one. It suggests something about what makes meaning possible: an individual must share large parts of her language with others in order to have one to begin with. (This is reminiscent of the sceptical solution; but recall that, as most readers agree, it is not viewed in this way by Wittgenstein, who is better seen as recommending that the sceptical problem be dissolved, and thus certainly not as denying that ascriptions of meaning can be true.) As for agreement in judgements, it is presumably required for making agreement in meaning possible. Presumably the agreement in question is to be understood as agreement in basic judgements. Thus we could not agree with others that we mean *green* by 'green', and hence we could not mean *green* by 'green', if we did not agree in the judgement 'This green blouse is the same colour as that green sweater'; we could not agree with others that we mean +2 by '+2', and hence we could not mean +2 by '+2', if we did not agree in the judgement 'When writing down the series +2, writing 1,002 after 1,000 is going on in the same way as writing down 1,000 after 998.'

What Wittgenstein also maintains is that the way we mean things by our words is 'exhibited' in the ways we distinguish between their correct and incorrect applications. This is to remind us of the essential connection there is between words' meaning what they do and their having the standards of correct use they have. From this connection it follows that for language users to agree on what they mean by their words is for them to agree on what the standards of correctness are that govern the uses of their words. But this is not to say that their agreeing on the correctness of a use makes the use correct; they only agree on what it takes for it to be correct – for example, for one's use of 'green' in 'Julie's blouse is green' to be correct, one must mean *green* by 'green' and Julie's blouse must be green. Still, it is through their use that standards somehow emerge. It might then be asked: how is this supposed to work? And the quietist will reply: what is the problem? As I see it, it is this.

The source of the problem is not hard to discern. On the one hand, language users must somehow establish the standards governing the uses of their words. Given that these standards are not to be provided through mere association with dead things and, in particular, given that people's uses – non-semantically characterized as mere bodily movements, productions of sounds and marks – are compatible with their meaning different things by the same words, people must somehow take their words to have the meanings and standards of correct use they have. However, on the other hand, the standards that they establish must also be objective; whether they are met or not must be independent of the fact that anyone or any group of people deems them to be so. To repeat once more a point I kept emphasizing in the previous chapter, if they were so dependent, there would be no distinction between correct and incorrect uses. Whatever use someone or some group of people would deem to be correct or incorrect would be correct or incorrect, so that no use would be meaningful. But then we seem to have a problem. On the one hand, if people have to establish the standards that govern the uses of their words, these standards are dependent on people's uses. On the other hand, in order to be objective, these standards must be independent of people's uses. How can we have it both ways? (Not to mention the related worry: if uses set the standards of correct use, how can any uses be incorrect, and, if only some uses do set these standards, which are they supposed to be?) This is a new puzzle for the philosopher of language to resolve, and its resolution may motivate some constructive, albeit still non-reductionist theorizing about meaning. I turn to an instance of such theorizing, which is inspired in part by Wittgenstein, who strongly suggested that a socially isolated individual could not draw an objective line between correct and incorrect uses of words – this is the second of his remarks that can be construed as encouraging non-quietism.

7.3   A non-reductionist account of meaning

Addressing the puzzle I find in Wittgenstein's remarks requires that we first address another problem, one that is faced by any externalist view of meaning, though it is a problem that, among the externalists we have discussed, only Davidson eventually addressed head-on.

Recall that, on the basis of the radical interpretation thought experiment, Davidson's initial assumption that meaning is to be understood in externalist terms was confirmed as well as further developed and refined. Recall that the externalism he advocated is different from other versions in three important respects: it is grounded on connections between sentences and what in the world makes them true rather than on connections between words and the external items they are about; it is thoroughly holistic; and, as a result, it prevents incomplete understanding of one's words from being pervasive. Thus, in some respects at least, Davidson's externalism was an improvement on other versions. Still, as it stood at the end of radical interpretation, it did leave us with a problem, which Davidson attempted to solve in the 1990s, in a series of papers that eventually outnumbered the papers on radical interpretation.

According to Davidson's externalism, the meanings of basic utterances such as 'There is a rabbit' are determined, at least in part, by their typical causes, that is, by the features of their environment that speakers are able to perceive and that typically cause them to produce those utterances. (The claim also applies to the contents of propositional thoughts and attitudes, contents that, as we saw when discussing radical interpretation, come to be determined together with the meanings of utterances.) The problem left over is this: how are the *typical* causes of a speaker's responses to her environment isolated? Just how does she come to distinguish among several aspects of the environment that may cause her utterances? For instance, just how does the cause of her responding 'rabbit' come to be rabbits rather than furriness, or fastness, or cuteness, so that she means *rabbit* by 'rabbit' rather than *furry* or *fast* or *cute*? Davidson thinks that a solitaire, someone who has grown up and always lived in social isolation, could not make these distinctions. He goes even further: a solitaire could not distinguish between proximal causes, causes that are in some way inside her, such as the stimulations of her nerve endings, and distal causes, causes that are outside her, such as objects and events around her, or anything to be found between proximal and such distal causes, or beyond the distal causes she perceives as she responds to them. Call the first problem the aspect problem and the second one the distance problem.

Let us leave aside the distance problem. Noticeably, this is a problem the radical interpreter does not have to solve. If the alien speaker can be understood, it is because the features of the environment she is responding to at the time when the interpreter is trying to understand her play a role in determining what she means by her words. The interpreter has to assume that the causes of the speaker's utterances are not only distal but are items they both are perceiving. But how does the interpreter get to determine what are the aspects of the distal causes the speaker is responding to? The interpreter cannot just assume that the speaker is responding to the aspects that she, the interpreter, would respond to. For one thing, the first time the speaker is responding it is certainly indeterminate what cause she is responding to. At the very least, in order to isolate the relevant aspect, the interpreter needs her to respond several times to similar causes. But what determines that a cause is similar to another? Any set of causes has 'endless properties in common', as Davidson points out. For another thing, assuming that the speaker is responding to the same aspects as the interpreter would respond to may be fine, but making this observation is not very illuminating at this stage; for what we want to know is how the relevant aspects of the causes of a speaker's responses are singled out to begin with, that is, how they are singled out by the speaker herself. To be told that the speaker does whatever the interpreter does does not tell us how the speaker got there, as it does not tell us how the interpreter did. We want to know how the aspect problem can be solved for a would-be speaker, and so what makes it possible for her to become a speaker.

A key to the solution to the problem is to acknowledge that, if the radical interpreter were to interact linguistically with the speaker, then presumably, little by little, the relevant aspects of the causes of the speaker's responses could be isolated. This, in essence, captures Davidson's solution. According to him, only someone who has responded to, and been responded to by, at least one other person, while both were also responding to common items in their environment, could have a language. Importantly, these mutual and simultaneous responses must have been linguistic, which makes the account circular – though, as we'll see once we understand the reasons for this claim, circular not in a vicious way: the account does not just say that only someone who has used a language could have a language. The basic claim already says quite a bit more: only someone who has interacted linguistically with at least one other person about shared features of their environment could have a language. Davidson uses the word 'triangulation' to label this kind of interaction, as the idea is that the interaction includes three vertices: the two speakers and the common item they are responding to. In fact there is a kind of triangulation that non-linguistic animals may engage in, as when two lionesses trying to catch a gazelle are coordinating their behaviour by watching each other and the gazelle and reacting to each other's reactions. Davidson says that the lionesses may rightly be described as reacting to the gazelle; the distance problem is solved – the cause of their reactions is 'the nearest mutual cause', to be found at the intersection of the two lines that may be drawn from each participant in the interaction. However, the lionesses cannot be said to have the concept of a gazelle. To have this concept and thus to mean *gazelle* by 'gazelle', one has to solve the aspect problem. And, to solve this problem, one needs to triangulate linguistically. But why?

To answer this question, it helps to start by asking just what predicament the solitaire is in. What needs first to be stressed is that, though features of the environment that cause one to react in certain ways play a role in determining what one means by one's words, these features do not come with a label written on them that would indicate what meaning they are determining. Objects and events in one's environment are (semantically speaking) as dead as the many individual items we considered in the previous chapter, and the idea that merely associating them with words could endow these words with meaning is as hopeless as the idea that merely associating words with individual items could endow these words with meaning. One must take an external item in a certain way, see it under a certain aspect, for the item to play a role in determining what one means by the word that refers to it. One must in effect tell which aspect it is that causes one's responses to it. This is to say that one must in effect tell which causes of one's responses are the same as which, which responses are objectively correct and which incorrect. As I said earlier, to establish meanings is to establish standards of correctness, and these have to be objective. Thus, to establish them, one must have the idea that there is an objective distinction between what is correct and what merely seems to be correct – call this idea the concept of objectivity. According to Davidson (who takes himself to be following Wittgenstein here), the main problem for the solitaire is that she could not be in a position to have this idea. That is, we could make no sense of how she could be. However, this changes dramatically if we think of someone as having triangulated linguistically.

According to Davidson, as I understand him, what makes it possible for individuals who triangulate linguistically to have the concept of objectivity is that they can engage in disputes about items in the environment surrounding them and, most importantly, they can settle their disputes in ways that are not exclusively dependent on one or the other interlocutor, as would be the case for a solitaire. Thus, suppose that two individuals have been spotting rabbits that gathered every day in some particular corner of the field around them. One day, on their evening walk, our two individuals fail to find the rabbits, upon which one of them declares 'We took the wrong turn', and the other 'The rabbits are gone.' Eventually they do settle their disagreement by determining whether they are really in the spot in which they observed the rabbits previously, for instance by recognizing some other feature of that spot. The main point here is that the settlement of the dispute is the product of a back-and-forth between them about an environment they share and that constrains their responses. The dispute is not settled simply on the basis of one or the other individual's view of the matter. Crucially, then, this kind of exchange makes room for the realization that their responses to the world may be correct or incorrect, and that they may be so objectively, as they are constrained by their environment. Nothing of the sort is possible for the solitaire. Even if we imagined her having a 'dispute' with herself, its 'resolution' would depend only on her own say.

It is also through this kind of back-and-forth between interlocutors about common items in their environment that the meanings of their words come to be fixed. Consider a child who is acquiring a first language. Initially she may apply the word 'cat' to all kinds of furry, four-legged, and cute things – dogs, cats, rabbits, and so on. Her caregivers will prompt her with questions – where is the cat, is there a cat in the bush, is Hector a cat or a dog . . .? And they will praise the child when she answers correctly and correct her when she does not. Eventually, through this process, the child will typically come to mean *cat* by 'cat'. I say 'typically' because, if she were to persist in using her word differently from her caregivers, she would end up meaning something different by the same word. Either way, what will in part determine the meaning of her word is the aspect of the world that she and her caregivers have agreed determines it. In short, then, it is the aspects that triangulating speakers have agreed are the aspects that contribute to determining the meanings of one another's words that do contribute to determining the meanings of one another's words.

Let me emphasize how different the situation here is from that of the sceptic's interlocutor envisaged by Kripke. Insofar as how the speaker uses her words was considered as a candidate for what determines what she means by them, this use was to be characterized in non-semantic terms, as the use of words to do something non-linguistic, such as getting a green object or calculating, rather than the use of words to say, or assert, or order – in short, to mean – things such as *green* by 'green' or *plus* by 'plus'. Furthermore, this use was to be thought of as the use of a single individual. Crucially, according to the Davidsonian account, the relevant use is shared, as it is shared use that allows for the isolation of the aspects of the world around us that contribute to determining the meaning of our words. And the relevant use can only be described in semantic terms, as the use of words to mean things. The positive story that is being given is that of what makes it possible for the use of words to be meaningful. Three further comments are in order here.

First, as already suggested, speakers do not have to mean the same things by the same words in order to mean anything by them. Of course, given the way the meanings of their words are determined, through collaborating with others and responding to features of the environment they share, there is bound to be a lot of overlap in what they mean by their words. At the same time, human relations being as complex as they are, there are bound to be a lot of idiosyncrasies as well. Second, the determination of what one means by one's words can occur only in a holistic way (as was the case in radical interpretation). Words need to be used on several occasions, in several contexts, and in several combinations, for the aspects of the world that contribute to determining their meaning to be isolated. Third, to say that meaning determination requires triangulation is not to say that, for every word that refers to an external object or event, one must have triangulated on the object or event in order to mean anything by the word that refers to it. To mean anything by one's words, one must only have triangulated on some objects and events; the meaning of other words can then be explained on the basis of those acquired through triangulation. But triangulation is necessary, as the shared world is the source of meaning, and can be understood as such only if one is in a position to distinguish objectively between correct and incorrect uses of words. Importantly, the determination of meanings does not precede the possession of the concept of objectivity. On the one hand, in order to isolate the aspects of the world that in part determine the meanings of one's words, one needs to have the concept of objectivity. On the other hand, in order to have the concept of objectivity, one needs to engage in linguistic disputes with others. Thus the two achievements are simultaneous. This is part and parcel of the limitations of the account. I turn to these limitations next, after articulating the positive claims the account affords.

7.4 The pros and cons of the non-reductionist account

According to this account, language is essentially social, though the kind of social externalism it advocates is different from that advocated by conventionalists such as Burge, encountered in chapter 4, and from the social view put forward by Kripke on the sceptic's behalf. For it does not maintain that what one means by one's words essentially depends on what the members of one's community mean by them. (Note that this is not to deny that linguistic conventions are widespread and useful; it is only to deny that they are essential to language.) But, contra Burge and Kripke, the account does maintain that communication with others, though possibly not meaning quite the same things by the same words, is essential to meaning anything by one's words, and thus to having a language. (Burge leaves it open that a solitaire could have a language; his view applies only to individuals who are socially situated. So does Kripke; he simply insists that the solitaire's language would have to be that of the community that is considering her.) The physical side of Davidson's externalism is also different from Putnam's physical externalism in that (in addition to the differences recalled earlier) it is essentially connected to the social side: only through social interactions do the aspects of the physical causes that in part determine meaning get isolated.

Interestingly, the account sheds some light on what Wittgenstein might have meant when he insisted that language rests on agreement in definitions and judgements. Expressed agreement between a speaker and at least one other person on what the speaker means by some of her words – which requires their agreeing in some judgements on which aspects of the world around them are the same as which – is needed for the speaker to mean anything. But disagreement, too, is needed for the speaker to have the requisite concept of objectivity, which enables her to distinguish between correct and incorrect uses of words, and to do so in an objective way. Thus, though it is speakers who, in part, establish the standards governing the uses of their words, these standards are also objective. Speakers recognize that they are established against the constraints of the world they share and that this world is independent of them. They are thus also in a position to recognize that, once standards are established, whether they are met or not is independent of any speaker's say. In short, the problem that, I suggested, remained for the non-reductionist – the problem of reconciling the fact that speakers somehow establish standards with these standards' being objective – is solved, though the solution rests on a distinction between two senses in which standards can be said to be objective. On the one hand, standards are not objective in the sense of existing altogether independently of us. This was to be expected, as we contribute to fixing them. They are the standards they are as a result of our using words the way we do. But, once standards are established, they, together with the world, constrain our future uses of words. In this sense, standards are objective and independent of us, that is, are met or not independently of our deeming them to be so.

As for the two conditions the sceptic challenged us to meet, that the account at least make room for the distinction between correct and incorrect uses of words and for the distinction between intelligent and robotic uses, it seems that they are met. On the one hand, standards of correct use are provided in the first place through people's use of words in communication with others about features of their environment they perceive and react to together. On the other hand, establishing these standards is accomplished through speakers' understanding others, and themselves, as producing utterances that are correct or incorrect – an understanding that is perforce intelligent and not merely robotic. I would rather not call this answer to the sceptic a straight solution, however, insofar as the sceptic's demand relied on a purely associative conception of meaning. Here the association of words with aspects of the world is only part of the story. Uses of words to communicate with others in triangulating interactions is the other important part. Finally, the account is compatible with maintaining that to mean something by a word is to be in a certain irreducible mental state of meaning, where this is understood not as having a finite object in one's mind, as Kripke envisioned, but as having a capacity, that of using the word in meaningful utterances, including in responses to the world that are correct or incorrect, and also a capacity of deeming an indefinite number of uses to be correct or not.

Yet is the account genuinely satisfactory?

The main problem with the account is that it is ultimately circular, which is to be expected, as it is a non-reductive account: it does not fully answer the question what it is for words to mean what they do exclusively in non-semantic terms, without relying at all on the very notion of meaning. Ultimately, to mean what one does by one's words is to have used them meaningfully, having taken at least some of them to apply correctly to features of one's environment. It may in fact be wondered what makes this view superior to what I have called the associative view, which I accused of incoherence, since, according to both views, one needs a language in order to be able to identify what is supposed to provide one's words with meaning to begin with. I think that there are two important differences between the non-reductionist view under consideration and the associative views rejected by the sceptic. First, the non-reductionist view does not maintain that words come to have meaning through *sheer* association with dead facts or things – in this case, items in the world around us. True, a kind of associating is taking place, but what the view articulates, which the sceptic's could not, is what makes those associations successful, that is, capable of fixing objective standards of correct use. And the reason why the sceptic could not stems from a significant difference between our non-reductionist's candidate determinants of meaning and the sceptic's: only the former's, items external to us, can be shared and triangulated upon – which, as we saw, allows speakers to isolate the relevant aspects of the external items that in part determine the meanings of their words. Internal items such as mental images or grasped senses are accessible to no one but the owner of these items, and they cannot therefore be disambiguated.

As for the circularity of the account, as I said earlier, it is inevitable, but it is not vicious. After all, if the account is right, what it has established is not exactly platitudinous: the essentially social character of language, as well as the essential role played by the environment of speakers, and hence the essential connection between meaning and truth. But these conditions – that in order to have a language one must interact with others and with the world they share, as well as have the concept of objectivity – are only necessary conditions for the possibility of language, that is, as I understand 'necessary', conditions that we need to invoke in order to make some sense of that possibility. According to this account, there is no fully instructive answer to the question how we go from having no language to having one, in that no instructive sufficient conditions can be given to explain in virtue of what a word means what it does – say, in virtue of what 'green' means *green*. All that can be said is that one uses the word to mean what it does, say, *green* by 'green' (though, to repeat, quite a bit has been said about what makes this kind of use possible). Some might protest that the 'magic' of language has not been fully elucidated. Others might conclude that there is no magic, just an irreducible, fundamental fact of human nature.

7.5 Epilogue

We have reached the end of our journey together. It is now for you, the reader, to continue it. One constant element of the views we have examined has been their focus on the descriptive aspect of language use. This was to be expected, especially from externalist views, as they emphasize the connections between language and what there is, or what is the case, in the environment of speakers. From describing the world, it is a short step to wishing it, hoping it, fearing it to be a certain way, and so on. That is, the various attitudes we may have towards a content do not change the meaning of the sentence that expresses it. If I say 'I hope the sun will shine tomorrow', I am not describing a state of affairs but hoping for one; but the meaning of the sentence expressing my hope is the same as the meaning of the description I express with 'The sun will shine tomorrow.' There are, however, many other ways in which we use language that might suggest that the literal meaning of a sentence may sometimes change, or that some additional or different kind of meaning is being expressed. Examples of these are metaphorical language – for example 'Juliet is the sun' – or ironical language – for example 'That was a clever thing to do' (to someone who just broke a glass) – or offensive language – for example 'She is a slut.'

What is it that makes a use of language metaphorical, or ironical, or offensive? Can what we have learned about language help us to understand those other uses? Are there principled ways of understanding them? Or should we follow here in the quietist's footsteps and conclude that the best we can do is to describe the multifarious, often unpredictable uses of language? Wondering about this is one way you might continue the journey on your own.

References

Davidson, Donald. 2001 [1992]. 'The Second Person', in his *Subjective, Intersubjective, Objective*. Oxford University Press, 107–121.

Davidson, Donald. 2001 [1997]. 'The Emergence of Thought', in his *Subjective, Intersubjective, Objective*. Oxford University Press, 123–134.

Davidson, Donald. 2001. 'Externalisms', in Petr Katatko, Peter Pagin, and Gabriel Segal (eds), *Interpreting Davidson*. Center for the Study of Language and Information, 1–16.

Wittgenstein, Ludwig. 2009 [1953]. *Philosophical Investigations* (4th edn), edited by P. M. S. Hacker and

Joachim Schulte, translated by G. E. M. Anscombe, P. M. S. Hacker, and Joachim Schulte. Wiley Blackwell.

Further Readings

Two good introductions to Wittgenstein:

Child, William. 2011. *Wittgenstein*. Routledge.

McGinn, Marie. 1997. *Wittgenstein and the Philosophical Investigations*. Routledge.

On semantic quietism:

McDowell, John. 2009. 'Wittgensteinian "Quietism"'. *Common Knowledge*, 15(3): 365–372.

Stroud, Barry. 2000. *Meaning, Understanding, and Practice*. Oxford University Press.

On Davidson's triangulation argument:

Davidson, Donald. 2001. *Subjective, Intersubjective, Objective*. Oxford University Press.

Myers, Robert H. and Claudine Verheggen. 2016. *Donald Davidson's Triangulation Argument: A Philosophical Inquiry*. Routledge.

On meaning and agreement:

Shaw, James R. 2023. *Wittgenstein on Rules: Justification, Grammar, and Agreement*. Oxford University Press.

Wittgenstein, Ludwig. 1983 [1956]. *Remarks on the Foundations of Mathematics* (rev. edn), edited by G. E. M. Anscombe, R. Rhees, and G. H. von Wright, translated by G. E. M. Anscombe. MIT Press.

On the degree to which language is conventional and the degree to which the meanings of our words are determined by the contexts in which we utter them:

Cappelen, Herman and Ernie Lepore. 2005. *Insensitive Semantics*. Blackwell.

Davidson, Donald. 2005 [1986.] 'A Nice Derangement

of Epitaphs'. *Truth, Language, and History*. Oxford University Press, 89–107.

Lewis, David. 2002 [1969]. *Convention*. Blackwell.

Ludlow, Peter. 2014. *Living Words*. Oxford University Press.

Recanati, Francois. 2004. *Literal Meaning*. Cambridge University Press.

Two introductory books on the questions concerning various kinds of non-standard and unethical uses of language:

Cappelen, Herman and Josh Dever. 2019. *Bad Language*. Oxford University Press.

Maitra, Ishani and Mary Kate McGowan. 2025. *Words in Action: An Introduction to the Social Philosophy of Language*. Oxford University Press.

On metaphor:

Camp, Elisabeth. 2006. 'Contextualism, Metaphor, and What Is Said'. *Mind & Language*, 21(3): 280–309.

Fogelin, Robert J. 2011. *Figuratively Speaking* (rev. edn). Oxford University Press.

Romero, Esther and Belén Soria. 2021. 'Philosophy of Language and Metaphor'. In Piotr Stalmaszczyk (ed.), *The Cambridge Handbook of the Philosophy of Language*. Cambridge University Press, 639–658.

On slurs and derogatory language (in addition to Cappelen and Dever, 2019 and Maitra and McGowan, 2025):

Camp, Elisabeth. 2013. 'Slurring Perspectives'. *Analytic Philosophy*, 54(3): 330–349.

Hornsby, Jennifer. 2001. 'Meaning and Uselessness: How to Think about Derogatory Words'. *Midwest Studies in Philosophy*, 25(1): 128–141.

Index